The concepts of illness,
disease and morbus

The concepts of illness, disease and morbus

F. KRÄUPL TAYLOR

*Emeritus Physician of the Bethlem Royal
and Maudsley Hospitals, London*

CAMBRIDGE UNIVERSITY PRESS

Cambridge
London   New York   Melbourne

Published by the Syndics of the Cambridge University Press
The Pitt Building, Trumpington Street, Cambridge CB2 1RP
Bentley House, 200 Euston Road, London NW1 2DB
32 East 57th Street, New York, NY 10022, USA
296 Beaconsfield Parade, Middle Park, Melbourne 3206, Australia

First published 1979

616.071
T34H

Printed in Great Britain
by W & J Mackay Limited, Chatham

Library of Congress Cataloguing in Publication Data
Taylor, Frederick Kräupl.

The concepts of illness, disease and morbus.

Includes index.

1. Diseases—Causes and theories of causation. I. Title.
RB151.T23   616.07'1   78-15123
ISBN 0-521-22433-0

To my wife Natalie

Venienti occurrite morbo, . . . discite, o miseri, et causas cognoscite rerum.
(Meet the morbus at its onset, . . . Learn, you unfortunates, and understand the causes of things.)

Persius, *Satires* III, 64 & 66

Contents

vii

Acknowledgements

I wish to thank Professor Robert H. Cawley for his helpful remarks on a previous version of this book, when it still contained an abundance of logical formulae which would have been indigestible to a medical readership. My thanks are also due to Professor Stephan Körner who was kind enough to read this book in its almost final version. He has given me sound advice on the logical background of my argument. He is, however, not responsible for any formulations I finally chose as I wished to keep clear of many of the complexities and perplexities of logical thought in the interest of a presentation which, I hope, will be understandable to persons who are not versed in the special terminology of logical discourse.

Early notions of disease

It has always been common knowledge that a person can fall ill after sustaining an injury in battle or through accident, fire, poison, and the like. Whenever this happens, there is no doubt about the reason for the disease of that person. But people – as well as animals and plants – can also develop a disease without any readily discernible reason. Such unaccountable misfortunes have always caused bewilderment and unease. People want to know, for their own comfort and peace of mind, why and how troubles come to pass so that they can hope to find suitable measures of prevention and alleviation.

The most acceptable explanations of disease or of any other misfortune have always been in terms of causes. Ideas of causality are firmly rooted in our minds. They may spring from our constant experience that we ourselves can function as the causes of events. We can will a movement and execute it, thus setting in train a whole series of effects. Notions of causality form very early in the minds of infants. Piaget (1955) found evidence of their occurrence as early as eighteen months after birth. Explanations based on concepts of causality therefore come easily to us and they must have come more easily still to pre-scientific generations who viewed the world as being governed by supernatural powers, usually endowed with human mentality, even when they were given monstrous and frightening shapes.

When the causes of disease are not obvious, they may be

1

thought of as invisible agents which affect our bodies by stealth. As Berghoff (1947), for instance, has pointed out, such causes are often pictured in primitive societies as sins against divine commandments or social taboos. It was also a habit of primitive thought to reify its ideas and thus consider them as akin to concrete objects which, though imperceptible, have an independent existence of their own and an independent power of transforming a healthy person into a disease-ridden patient. Before such patients could be helped, the kind of sin responsible had to be diagnosed. This was a job for experts, such as priests, soothsayers, and medicine men. Their expertise was supposed to include also the knowledge of how to get rid of the diagnosed sin. In their *materia medica*, they had available such dispensations as sacrificial offerings and rites of expiation and purification.

When sins are reified, they can be viewed as freely roaming the world so that they can be acquired by a malefactor and perhaps even those around him. Beliefs in the sinfulness of disease are so deeply ingrained in our culture that they are still with us. They have merely adopted new theoretical guises and hidden their identity behind pseudonyms. Towards the end of the nineteenth century, for instance, there was a kind of sin that was known as degeneracy. It could be acquired through reckless indulgence in too much alcohol, sex, or loose and perverted living; it could be passed on to offspring, as though to fulfil the ancient prophecy that the sins of fathers are visited upon their children. The notion of degeneracy was thus tinged with moral disparagement and regarded as beyond medical competence. In the less moralistic climate of today, the sin of degeneracy has disappeared from our diagnostic

2

vocabulary, though not from our aetiological considerations. It has merely found refuge in more mundane theories.

What is still with us is the idea that patients are to blame for some of their diseases, especially those which originate in some gratifying pleasure, such as smoking, over-eating, drunkenness, drug abuse, lack of physical exercise (the ancient sin of sloth), and the like. Only masturbation has recently been removed from the list of pathogenic activities. What is also still with us is the idea that patients can be the innocent victims of faults that lie elsewhere. Blame has been attached to parental stock, family life, and social conditions. It has been attached to parental stock when genetic sources have been shown to be the chief matrix of a disease; it has been attached to early family life by Freud and his followers in the case of neurotic and psychopathic diseases; and it has been attached to social conditions by the zeal of social reformers and the studies of sociologists. The notion of sin has thus been converted into concepts that have a more pragmatic basis.

The sins of ancient times were, however, not always regarded as being pathogenic agents in their own right. They were often pictured as merely having the function of rousing the wrath of deities who had it in their power to punish culprits and their communities, unless they saved themselves by timely penitence and self-imposed suffering. Among their punishments was the infliction of disease.

It would be an oversimplification, however, to maintain that all causes of disease were thought of as related to sins. It was also believed that other noxious agents were about in the world which could afflict persons who happened to be around. Many of these agents were assumed to be tied to particular places, to flourish in particular climates, or to make their appearance at particular seasons of the year.

To the question of how noxious agents, whether they were sins or not, were related to the disease symptoms which patients exhibited, two answers could be given, though they were not mutually contradictory. According to one kind of answer, the symptoms were for the most part attributes of the noxious agent as it developed in the body of the patient. This view gave rise to theories of disease which were called 'ontological'. The alternative answer was that the symptoms were mainly bodily reactions evoked by the noxious agent. This view gave rise to what may be called the 'reactive' theories of disease.

2

Ontological theories of disease

Ontological theories concern themselves with the question of what exists as entities in some realm. Philosophers have wrangled with these theories and have arrived at the most diverse solutions. Their disagreements are still reflected in the variety of meanings that can be given to the term 'entity'. Among the definitions of the term given by Webster's *Third New International Dictionary of the English Language* (1971) are the following: 'something that has independent or separate existence, . . . something that has a unitary and self-contained character'. Concrete objects and events can therefore be regarded as entities as long as their independent or separate individuality and unity lasts. The term can also be used in an abstract sense. It then signifies 'an abstraction, ideal conception, object of thought' which is viewed as a singularity, even though it may be of complex composition.

The noxious disease agents of ancient beliefs could be concrete natural entities, such as miasmata, effluvia, and malodorous emanations of various sorts; they could be concrete supernatural entities, such as demons, furies, spirits, and the like; or they could be reified abstract entities, such as sins, curses, or spells. The model for these entities was plant seeds which could be minute and invisible. Yet in the right kind of soil and under suitable conditions plant seeds could grow into very noticeable organisms with characteristic attributes. In the same way, it was thought, could a

5

disease entity grow in the body of a patient and develop characteristic attributes which could be noticed as symptoms. Disease entities were thus credited with having an almost independent existence. They could even leave a patient's body again in order to affect and plague other people.

The myths and legends of mankind freely postulated the presence in the world of such independent disease entities. We find references to them in the Bible, for example, when the Lord was said to have sent out the disease entities of boils, plagues, and other pestilences in order to punish Pharaoh. Another instance is the Greek story of Pandora, the first woman. Zeus created her to penalize mankind for accepting the gift of divine fire which Prometheus had stolen from Olympus. Pandora was given a box containing the forbears of all diseases, of 'all the Spites that might plague mankind: such as Old Age, Labour, Sickness, Insanity, Vice, and Passion' (Graves, 1955, Vol. 1, p. 145).

This age-old ontological interpretation of disease has become so deeply embedded in our language that we readily use idioms with ontological implications that are conveniently overlooked, at least in everyday speech. Usually, we do not give it a second thought, when we talk of 'catching' a disease, of being 'attacked' by it, 'struck' by it ('stroke', 'apoplexy'), 'seized' by it ('seizure', 'epilepsy'). We speak of disease 'carriers' who are not ill themselves, of diseases which are 'transmitted' from person to person or parent to child, which move as 'epidemics' from place to place or lurk as 'endemic' dangers waiting for the unimmunized traveller.

The ontological theory of disease was most clearly enunciated by Thomas Sydenham in the seventeenth century (cf.

Dewhurst, 1966). His views carried great weight with medical men because they admired him for his clinical astuteness and his introduction of the method of nosography. It was a method which emphasized the paramount importance of carrying out careful and detailed clinical observations in order to distinguish between different disease entities. It contributed greatly to the advance of medicine in the two centuries that followed. It has been only in recent times that the method has lost some of its lustre and significance because we can today amplify our diagnostic acumen by calling on the skills of specialists in laboratory procedures and the use of sophisticated machinery.

Sydenham did not apply the ontological theory to all diseases. As has been pointed out by Entralgo (1955, pp. 113ff), he distinguished between chronic and acute diseases. Chronic diseases, in his view, had their origin in unhealthy ways of living, eating, and drinking. Acute diseases, on the other hand, were due to the invasion of a person's body by atmospheric miasmata. These miasmata were Sydenham's disease entities. They developed in the fluid 'humours' of a body to reach their mature forms. To use Sydenham's words (1676) in their English translation from the Latin by Latham (1848, p. 19): 'The said humours become exalted into a substantial form or species'. This statement may sound quaint and perhaps even nebulous to modern readers. It is expressed in terms which reflect thoughts and theories that are alien to us. The term 'exalted' has its origin in the alchemical notion that substances can be raised to a higher status of maturation and refinement through arcane forces. The expression 'substantial form or species' may also be puzzling. Sydenham often compared a disease entity to a botanical species and therefore spoke of

7

'specific' diseases. He and his contemporaries understood by 'species' a 'substantial form or essence' which had been created by God and existed, as it were, in a Platonic realm that was of higher reality, permanence, and perfection than our physical world of the senses in which the ideal forms of species manifested themselves in imperfect and transient objects. Sydenham saw nothing wrong in remarking: 'Plant is a species'. Indeed this kind of remark was regarded as legitimate by many logicians of his time. To them, the word 'plant' in the remark quoted functioned as a so-called 'simple supposition'. In modern logic, such simple suppositions and their confusing implications have disappeared. Today, the remark would be phrased in strict logical idiom: 'A plant belongs to (is a member of) a species'.

Taking note of these peculiarities in the theoretical background of Sydenham's remarks, there should be no difficulty in appreciating the sense of further quotations which will clarify the tenor of his thought and teaching. 'Every specific disease is a disorder that originates from this or that exaltation. . . . Each juice has its exaltations as soon as it has broken out into a species. Of this we have a clear, visible, and daily proof in the different species of excrescences, which tree and fruit exhibit in the shape of moss, and mistletoe, and fungi, and the like. . . . These excrescences are, each and all, *essences or species wholly distinct and different from the parent stock*, whether tree or shrub.' (Latham, 1848, pp. 18f. Italics mine.)

It did not escape Sydenham that the diseases which developed in the bodies of patients did not, like other entities, have separate and independent existences. He admitted: 'I cannot deny that whereas all species, both of plants and animals, with the exception of a very few, subsist by themselves, the species of disease depend upon the humours that engender them' (Latham, 1848, p. 20). As Sydenham believed that disease entities were like plant species, he was convinced that they had a natural history, that they appeared at certain seasons of the year, grew to maturity and faded away again. Malaria, for example, had the following natural history: 'It begins almost always in autumn; it keeps to a regular course of succession; it preserves a definite type; its periodical revolutions, occurring on the fourth day, if undisturbed by external influences, are as regular as those of a watch or any other piece of machinery; it sets in with shivers and a notable feeling of cold, which are succeeded by an equally decided sensation of heat, and it is terminated by a most profuse perspiration. Whoever is attacked must bear with his complaint till the vernal equinox, there or thereabouts. Now putting all this together, we find reasons for believing that this disease is a species equally cogent with those that we have for believing a plant to be a species. The plant springs from the earth; the plant blooms; the plant dies; the plant does all this with equal regularity' (p. 19). We no longer believe today that diseases are like plants, yet we still speak of their 'natural history'.

For Sydenham, the diagnostic task of doctors consisted in distinguishing the various disease species which belong to the same disease genus and therefore have some characteristics in common, though they are different in essence. He remarked: 'It happens, at present, that many diseases, although included in the same genus, mentioned with a common nomenclature, and resembling one another in several symptoms, are, notwithstanding, different in their natures, and require different medical treatment' (p. 13). In other words, doctors used the same generic name for different disease species because they had not yet learned to differentiate them. It was like using the same word 'rose' for the great variety of wild and cultivated species in the genus *Rosa*. Sydenham insisted that 'in the first place, it is necessary that all diseases be reduced to definite and certain species, and that with the same care which we see exhibited by botanists in their phytologies' (p. 13). To achieve this, he recommended: 'In writing the history of a disease, every philosophical hypothesis whatsoever that had previously occupied the mind of the author, should lie in abeyance. This being done, the clear and natural phenomena of the disease should be noted accurately, and in all their minuteness. It is necessary, in describing any disease, to enumerate the peculiar and constant phenomena apart from the accidental and adventitious ones; these last-named being those that arise from the age or temperament of the patient, and from the different forms of medical treatment' (p. 14).

Once having isolated a disease species, there was a chance of finding remedies that were successful in its treatment because they were 'specifics' for that species. Quinine in the cinchona bark which Jesuits had brought back from Peru in Sydenham's time was such a specific in treating the disease species of malaria.

The enthusiasm with which the medical world welcomed Sydenham's recipe for unbiased and detailed clinical nosography was partly due to its iconoclastic merits. It propounded the importance of letting observed facts reign supreme over reliance on the dicta and doctrines of past medical authorities. It encouraged medical men to shake off the shackles of outdated text-book teaching and to embark on an independent search for new clinical data. It certainly

10

helped to speed medical progress along. Yet looking back, one has to admit that progress was of necessity limited as long as clinical observation was restricted to barehanded, or almost barehanded, bedside activities. Even today, with all the resources of modern technology at our disposal, we are still fully stretched in our continuing efforts to unravel tangles of similar diseases into separate nosological strands.

While Sydenham was thus given full credit for his nosographic method by later generations of physicians, his ontological theory of disease, by contrast, ran into a mixed and often hostile reception. In the middle of the nineteenth century, the young, impetuous, and militant Rudolf Virchow (cf. Ackerknecht, 1953 and Rather, 1959) vehemently denounced it. At the ripe age of 26 years, he founded, together with his friend B. Reinhardt, the medical journal which, in due course, acquired the title of *Virchow's Archiv*. In his inaugural article (1847), Virchow was outspoken in his categorical dismissal of the ontological theory of disease. 'Diseases', he said, 'have no independent or isolated existence; they are not autonomous organisms, not beings invading a body, nor parasites growing on it; they are only the manifestations of life processes under altered conditions'. The second volume of the *Archiv* (1849) began with another article by Virchow in which he repeated his conviction that 'there are no disease entities (*Krankheitsentitaeten*)'. (My translations.)

This was the voice of Virchow in his youth. At a later stage, his opinions underwent a *volte face*. He evolved his own ontological theory of disease which differed fundamentally from that of Sydenham. By that time, he had become the protagonist of pathological anatomy and a stout advocate of the cellular theory which maintained that biological cells were the building stones of all living organisms and whose motto was *omnis cellula e cellula*. The thesis of his book on Cellular Pathology (1858) was that life, in both its healthy and diseased forms, began and ended in cells. Under his leadership, pathological anatomists and histologists assumed the role of the final arbiters of clinical diagnoses. It was the function of clinicians to investigate their patients and to infer from their findings the kind of pathological lesions which were present anatomically; it was the function of the anatomical pathologist to establish the truth or falsehood of the clinicians' diagnostic inferences. In previous centuries, patients had been diagnosed according to their clinical manifestations as suffering from such maladies as fever, dropsy, jaundice, dyspepsia, paralysis, and the like. Now such clinical diagnostic labels were no longer acceptable; they had to be exchanged for pathological disease tags, announcing what was wrong anatomically.

When Virchow, at the age of 74 years, reviewed *One Hundred Years of General Pathology* (1895), he asserted: 'In my view, *a disease entity is an altered part of the body*; in principle, an altered cell or cell aggregate. . . . In this sense, I am a thoroughgoing ontologist and have always regarded it as a merit to have brought into harmony with genuine scientific knowledge the old and essentially justified assertion that *disease is a living entity that leads a parasitic existence*. Every diseased part of the body has indeed a parasitic relationship with the otherwise healthy body to which it belongs and at the expense of which it lives.' (My translation and italics.)

It was as though for Virchow a patient consisted of two entities: the original organismic entity and the acquired disease entity. The latter, however, did not come from the outside world; it had its origin and habitat in the body of a patient. It was composed of demonstrable pathological changes of a macroscopic and/or microscopic kind. A whole new nosology was thus established. For preference, each disease in it was given a Latin name that described the pathological changes of which it essentially consisted, e.g. cerebral tumour, pneumonia, mitral stenosis, gastric ulcer, hepatic cirrhosis, appendicitis, arthritis, and so on.

The differences between Sydenham's and Virchow's ontological views are significant pointers to some of the changes in medical and scientific outlook that had occurred in the intervening two centuries. Sydenham's disease entities had a supposedly humoral pathology; they were body-alien elements which developed in, and thus changed, the patient's humours. They became noticeable in the form of those clinical manifestations which were features of the disease entity and not of the bodily entity of the patient. Virchow's disease entities, on the other hand, had a solid pathology; they were assumed to originate in alterations in some of the patient's bodily cells. They became noticeable in the form of somatic changes in cells, organs, and tissues. These changes were the features which characterized a Virchowian disease entity and by which it was diagnosed. Sydenham was essentially a clinician; his knowledge of the body's pathological anatomy was of the scantiest kind, since Morgagni's great work that launched the new medical discipline of pathological anatomy was 85 years in the future, when Sydenham wrote the lines we quoted. Virchow, on the other hand, was essentially a pathological anatomist and histologist, at least in his medical role (his other roles being those of a prominent anthropologist and progressive politician). He left the evaluation of clinical data to the medical men who had direct contact with the living patients.

The intellectual conception of the world had also fundamentally changed between the seventeenth and nineteenth centuries. The seventeenth century was a deeply devout era whose wars were kindled by religious passions. Sydenham was a Puritan who interrupted his medical studies in Oxford in order to fight in Cromwell's cavalry. The nineteenth century was a materialistic age. It did not fight its political battles with the fanaticism of religious faith but with the fervour of social ideologies. Virchow was in the forefront of the new battles and, as a member of the Prussian Parliament and later the Berlin Reichstag, was well placed to pursue what he called his *Kulturkampf* which aimed at removing social injustices and unhygienic living conditions from the underprivileged masses.

The contrasts between the climates of beliefs in which Sydenham and Virchow lived were reflected in their ontological theories of disease in subtle and yet significant ways. For Sydenham and his contemporaries, a species was more 'real' in a metaphysical sense than any species member. What could be said about species members in our imperfect world had to be true to a much greater extent of the God-given perfect species. That is why Sydenham stated so nonchalantly that a disease or a plant is a species. In the reified sense given to it at that time, a species was something singular; only its members were manifold. A particular species thus commanded the definite article. When Molière, for example, lampooned the doctors of the seventeenth century in his *L'Amour Médecin* (1665), he made the seller of a quack medicine sing (in H. Baker and J.

14

Miller's translation, 1739; quoted from L. Clendening, 1942, pp. 227f):

> My remedy cures, by its excellence rare,
> More maladies than you can count in a year.
> > The scab,
> > The itch,
> > The scurf,
> > The plague,
> > The fever,
> > The gout,
> > The pox,
> > The flux,
> > And measles ever.

The disease entity that Virchow had in mind in the nineteenth century was much more down to earth. It was not a class entity such as a biological species is; it was a particular pathological abnormality in a particular patient. The same kind of pathological abnormality could, of course, also be found in other patients. To express this differently: the disease entity found in a patient was regarded as a member of a class of similar disease entities in other patients. Therefore, since a Virchowian disease entity was one of many, grammatically it required the indefinite article. A patient thus had *a* cerebral tumour, *a* pneumonia, *a* mitral stenosis, *a* gastric ulcer, and so on. Indeed from this point of view, two patients with, say, mitral stenosis could be said to have two disease entities of the same kind.

When Virchow stated that a disease entity was an altered part of the body, he began a process of changing the meaning of 'entity' in medicine. It no longer indicated something that had 'independent or separate existence', but something that was only part of a person and therefore dependent on and non-separate from him. It still was viewed, however, as having 'a unitary and self-contained character' and for that reason as an entity. Essentially, it was, however, an attribute of a person, namely that attribute which assigned him to the class of patients. But when we mention a particular attribute in an object or in a class of objects, we are at liberty to introduce that attribute with or without the indefinite article. There is only a linguistic embargo on the definite article in this context, at least in languages which possess definite and indefinite articles. It does not really matter much, whether we say that men of genius have 'a superior intelligence' or 'superior intelligence', or whether doctors have 'a professional status' or 'professional status'. Similarly, patients may be said to have 'brain tumour', 'pneumonia', 'mitral stenosis', 'gastric ulcer', and so on. The usages of language can be fair reflections of theoretical beliefs that prevail at different times and in different communities.

3

Reactive theories of disease

The reactive theories of disease are more thoroughly based on concepts of causality than are any of the ontological theories we have been considering so far. That is not to say that ontological theories completely neglect causality. They take it into account in the sense that they regard their disease entities as the causes of a patient's complaints. But their contention is that these causes are of a special kind because they are independent, or at least semi-independent, of a patient's body. Sydenham saw his disease entities as body-alien intruders which grew into mature forms in a patient's humours. Of course, they were credited with eliciting reactions from a patient's body, but such reactions could be interpreted as disease-countering and curative processes. Virchow's disease entities, on the other hand, were regarded as indigenous in a patient's body. They were thought of as bodily reactions to pathogenic causes, reactions which grew into pathological manifestations and set themselves up as parasitic opponents to the rest of the body. Causality considerations stopped for Virchow at the pathological level. Clinical consequences and aetiological antecedents were of only secondary interest to him. As far as he was concerned the sole business of medicine was to diagnose whatever pathological disease entity was present and to remove or contain it through medication or surgery, if this could be done without causing unacceptable harm.

The concepts of illness, disease and morbus

Virchow's special enmity was reserved for the then newly emerging medical discipline of bacteriology. He wrote angrily about 'the hopeless, never-ending confusion with which the ideas of being (*ens morbi*) and causation (*causa morbi*) have been arbitrarily mixed up' (1895, my translation). It is true that, in the first flush of enthusiasm, some bacteriologists overshot the mark and spoke as though bacteria were disease entities in Sydenham's sense. But when more sober reflections prevailed, they agreed with Virchow that pathogenic bacteria were merely the potential causes of pathological effects. Where they remained in conflict with him was in the area of diagnostic evaluation and nomenclature. In their opinion, medical diagnoses should, whenever possible, reflect the origin of pathological lesions and not merely indicate the kind of lesion present. For example, if tubercle bacilli were responsible for a pathological effect, the diagnosis should be tuberculosis irrespective of the particular kind of pathological effect caused.

Virchow found this kind of reasoning topsy-turvy. Since he began with the premise that a pathological abnormality constituted a disease entity, the diagnosis had to name the abnormality, no matter how it was caused. For example, if there were non-caseating tubercles composed of epitheloid cells in the body of a patient, he suffered from the disease entity of tuberculosis. Of course, tubercle bacilli could be responsible for the origin of that disease entity. But it could have other causes; for example, as we know today, it could be due to leprosy bacilli, brucella bacteria, histoplasma fungi, beryllium poisoning, or the unknown agent of sarcoidosis. If there were caseating lesions and cavities in the body of a patient, he suffered, according to Virchow, from a different disease entity, namely a decaying disease, or

18

phthisis. It was not the same disease entity as tuberculosis, even if it was due to tubercle bacilli, because its pathological characteristics were different. Virchow advanced the same kind of argument in other contexts. Diphtheria, for example, was to him a disease entity that was characterized by surface necrosis and membrane formation in an organ. It could be due to diphtheria bacilli, but could just as well have other causes.

From a logical point of view, Virchow's argument is perfectly correct, once one has accepted his first premise. Presented in the form of a syllogism, his argument is:

> All patients with pathological tubercles in their bodies suffer from tuberculosis.
> This patient has pathological tubercles in his body.
> _____
> Therefore this patient suffers from tuberculosis.

But Virchow's first premise is not sacrosanct. Other premises are possible and equally correct, though different, inferences can be drawn from them. In syllogistic form, the reasoning of bacteriologists would look like this:

> All patients with pathological lesions caused by tubercle bacilli suffer from tuberculosis.
> This patient has pathological lesions caused by tubercle bacilli.
> _____
> Therefore this patient suffers from tuberculosis.

For practical reasons, the premises of the bacteriologists have been found more acceptable to medical men than those of Virchow. These premises are not restricted to infectious diseases. They imply a principle that is applicable to all

19

diseases, namely the principle of tracing back a pathological chain of events beyond the occurrence of Virchowian disease entities to the first endogenous causes responsible for them, to their *pathological onset* as I shall say. Such a pathological onset may be the arrival in a patient's body of pathogenic organisms or of some physical or chemical damage; it may be the presence of pathological genes or chromosomal aberrations in a zygote; it may be any kind of noxious influence to which a person is exposed in his life. However, a pathological onset does not invariably give rise to a full-blown disease. Development may be halted at an early stage by the body's defences or some prophylactic treatment. A pathological predisposition may also arise, that is a pathological reactivity which lies dormant until an intercurrent event arouses it and precipitates an overt disease.

What is important from this point of view is that any disease events that derive from a particular kind of pathological onset acquire that unitary and self-contained character which has come today to be the main hallmark of an entity. Such disease events may thus be regarded as forming disease entities in a modern sense, namely *monogenic disease entities*.

A monogenic disease entity can, of course, comprise different Virchowian disease entities as we have already seen in the example, when the pathological onset was a tuberculous infection. It then depends on many contingencies what kind of Virchowian disease entities will follow from that kind of pathological onset. A modern monogenic disease entity is thus an abstract concept that is viewed as a singularity, though it is of multiple and manifold composition. Diagnosing a monogenic disease entity does not relieve us of the task of taking into account the particular forms it can take in particular instances.

Most diseases which are acknowledged in medicine today are certainly not monogenic disease entities. Yet the final hope and aim of medical science is the establishment of monogenic disease entities and that means the detection of pathological onsets and their causal consequences. Such detection is not only a task for practical investigations, it also requires a scrutiny of the principles of causality so that the various problems which can arise in causal analyses may be understood.

The principles of causality have undergone many theoretical changes in the course of time. In past centuries, it was believed that two kinds of causality exist. One kind was thought to be capricious and unpredictable, because it was at the mercy of fickle arcane powers; the other kind was thought of as subject to natural laws and therefore predictable in its processes.

The theories of capricious causality postulated the existence of beings with supernatural or magical craft at their disposal, such as the Fates, the Norns, Gods, Devils, sorcerers, and witches. They could wilfully bend the course of events in our world to suit their whims. The theories of lawful causality, on the other hand, relied on regularities and uniformities inaugurated, according to predilection, by God, Logos, or Nature. With the arrival of the scientific era in the seventeenth century, the theories of lawful causality won the day together with the hopeful belief that the human mind was capable of discovering natural laws and understanding how they worked. Until the end of the nineteenth century, the scientific credo was that all events in the natural world were inexorably determined, and thus predetermined and predestined, by mechanistic laws. Laplace (1814) gave expression to this conviction, when he said: 'Given for one instant an intelligence which could comprehend all the forces by which nature is animated and the respective situation of the beings who compose it – an intelligence sufficiently vast to submit these data to analysis – it would embrace in the same formula the movements of the greatest bodies of the universe and those of the lightest atom; for it, nothing would be uncertain and the future, as the past, would be present in its eyes.'

This credo was christened 'scientific determinism'. It implied that it was only the inadequacy of our knowledge and intelligence which prevented us from unravelling the past and predicting the future with complete certainty and assurance. It was only our intellectual shortcomings which confined us to a world full of uncertainties. Of course, the belief in scientific determinism clashed with our proud conviction that human beings have a free will and are the masters of their fate. If scientific determinism were entirely true, it would make us into mere puppets that move in automatic obedience to the immutable laws of causality. Moreover, once the reality of free will is denied, what becomes of moral responsibility? Deprived of the ultimate freedom to choose between good and bad, right and wrong, we can be neither sinners nor saints. We deserve no credit for our virtues and achievements nor blame for our wrongdoings and failures. Sir Karl Popper (1973, p. 217) has called this dilemma 'the nightmare of the physical determinist'. Fortunately for our peace of mind, the nightmare has been dispelled by modern developments in theoretical physics. It is now generally accepted that in the subatomic realm it is the uncertainty of quantum mechanics that prevails and not

the certainty of the laws of classical physics. This development was immediately welcomed by Sir Arthur Eddington
(1935, p. 284) because, as he put it, 'science thereby with-
draws its moral opposition to free will'. Munn (1960, p. 213),
in a wide-ranging analysis of free will and determinism has
come to a similar conclusion: 'Modern physics, while being
unable to prove that he [the commonsense man] has free-
will, at least now concedes the possibility'.

Scientific determinism had assumed that there is an
unbroken continuity between all events in this world, that
they merge into one another without breaks. It then seemed
plausible to postulate an inexorable link between a causal
event A and its immediately following effect B. Since B, in
its turn, would then become the causal event of its immediately following effect C, we would end up with an inevitable
causal chain. In this scheme of thought, every particular
event would be the 'sufficient' cause of its immediate effect,
i.e. it would be sufficient by itself to bring about the effect.
Similarly, every effect would have its immediate antecedent
as its 'necessary' cause, i.e. without the occurrence of that
cause the effect would not have happened.

The assumption of an unbroken continuity between
events has been shown to be invalid in the subatomic field,
where events are definitely discontinuous. For this and
other reasons, scientific determinism does not apply there.
It has, however, still some plausibility in our macroscopic
world, especially when it is applied to the working of some
simple machine or strictly controlled experimental set-up.
Its plausibility diminishes, when a wider context is considered. Causal chains cannot be viewed in isolation then, but
as individual elements in a welter of constantly interacting
causal chains. As a result, no single event can be regarded as

The concepts of illness, disease and morbus

the sufficient cause of an effect. An event A is the cause of the immediate effect B only in conjunction with favourable adjuvant circumstances whose composition may be, and often is, largely unknown. If those circumstances alter significantly, the immediate effect of event A will not be B. Any particular kind of event is thus the potential cause of a range of different immediate effects, and an even wider range of later effects. Each effect in the possible range will have its own probability of occurring, depending on the frequency with which its favourable adjuvant circumstances are present.

Applied to the concept of a monogenic disease entity, this means that a particular kind of pathological onset can have a wide range of effects which need not all be pathological ones. The range of effects is governed by adjuvant circumstances within and without the patient and by the length of time that has elapsed between the cause and its effects. For example, if the pathological onset is the presence of trisomy 21 in a human zygote, its effects are probably always detrimental, ranging from death before birth to various combinations of clinical manifestations out of a set of over forty possible abnormalities that have been observed in this monogenic disease entity which used to be known as 'mongolism' and is today usually called 'Down's syndrome' (cf. Penrose & Smith, 1966, Ch. 8). The presence of trisomy 21 in a human zygote is of high pathogenic power, because adjuvant circumstances are probably always such that deleterious consequences follow.

There are also pathological onsets whose pathogenic power is low. They have morbid consequences only in special adjuvant circumstances. An example is the presence in a human zygote of just one gene whose copies in eryth-

24

ropoietic cells code for haemoglobin S (HbS). A person with one such gene has up to 40% HbS in his erythrocytes and is said to have a sickle cell 'trait', not a sickle cell 'disease'. It is a trait that has morbid consequences only when unfortunate adjuvant circumstances obtain, such as low oxygen pressure in a high-flying aircraft, which can still be tolerated by other persons.

Pathological onsets are events which, like all other events in our macroscopic world, lie on interacting causal chains. They have antecedents which are events external to a person in space-time. Such events, considered by themselves, are potential noxae. They are potential, because they may not impinge on any particular person or any person at all. They occur in space-time, because they are either in a person's spatial environment or precede his existence in time. Among potential environmental noxae are catastrophes of all kinds, virulent micro-organisms, poisons, sharp-edged objects, the weapons of war, and the like. Among potential pre-existence noxae are pathogenic mutations or chromosomal maldistributions during meiotic processes in ancestral gonads.

Potential noxae can turn into actual noxae, when they impinge upon a person and cause a pathological onset. However, this depends on two factors: the pathogenic power of the noxa and the vulnerability of the person on whom the noxa impinges. Taking both factors into account, we can distinguish *unselective* and *selective noxae*. Among unselective noxae are the inheritance from both parents of the recessive genes for HbS, the inheritance from one parent of the dominant gene for Huntington's chorea, the infliction of such violence that fractures, contusions or open wounds result, the bite of a venomous snake, a virulent

25

infection, or over-exposure to excessive heat or cold or radioactivity. Among selective noxae are a heterozygous inheritance of the recessive gene for HbS which becomes pathogenic at low oxygen pressures, the inhalation of grass pollen which becomes pathogenic in pollen-allergic persons, the ingestion of gluten which becomes pathogenic in patients with coeliac disease, or the exposure to strong sunlight which becomes pathogenic in some patients with porphyric predispositions or on phenothiazine medication.

When we are dealing with unselective noxae, their impingement on the body gives rise to pathological onsets without fail. Those pathological onsets are occasionally Virchowian disease entities. This, for instance, is the case when a person receives a shot or stab wound. Other pathological onsets ripen gradually into an overt disease, because among the adjuvant circumstances in the body of the patient there are none which will put a stop to this development. Still other pathological onsets lead only to pathological predispositions which need as their activating complement a selective noxa of the right kind to precipitate a disease.

When scientific determinism was still in its heyday, the existence of necessary and inexorable bonds between a cause and its particular effect was generally postulated. But such bonds were not observable, except perhaps in a simple case of direct mechanical impact such as the collision between billiard balls. The non-observability of causal bonds was one of the reasons why determinism of this predestined kind came under philosophical attack. Hume led the vanguard of the attack as early as 1739 in his *Treatise of Human Nature*. He argued that the postulated bonds may have no counterparts in factual reality, that they are only ideas in the minds of men, that they are inferred from observations that 'one particular species of event has always, in all instances, been conjoined with another'. Yet the mere conjunction of two species of event did not permit such inferences. *Post hoc* was never a guarantee of *propter hoc*. After all, day follows night always and in all instances, and yet there is no direct causal link. Considerations of this nature eventually persuaded theoretical physicists that they might safely dispense with the deterministic concept of cause and replace it with the concept of functional relations between events, relations which can ultimately be expressed in formal equations. However, in practice, such formal theoretical equations always needed corrections and in any case, did not eliminate the concept of causality from practical thought. In modern theories, the principles of causality are no longer linked to deterministic postulates of inexorable bonds between cause and effect, but to postulates of energy transmissions and transformations. Like the concept of causal bonds, the concept of energy has its speculative aspects, especially as far as its constitution and provenance is concerned. But the practical manifestations of energy have the great advantage of being quantifiable.

When we consider the workings of any orderly and organized system, whether it be a man-made machine or some naturally occurring self-contained organization (e.g. a solar system, a biological organism, an ecological complex), causal relationships of some kind are always noticeable. The reason is that the orderly organization of those systems provides the adjuvant circumstances favouring particular causal relationships. In an unorganized and therefore chaotic system, causal relationships may seem to be absent. In such systems there is no regularity, so that an event of

27

kind A is only occasionally followed by an event of kind B. Yet even in a chaotic system, there is only a finite range of different kinds of events that can follow an event of kind A. For example, the throwing of a die initiates a chaotic system of events in which only six final events are possible. One of the six faces of the die will be uppermost when the die comes to rest and the chaotic system to an end. On the assumption that the chaos in the system is total, that there is no trace of order in it, each face of the die has the same chance of 1/6 of appearing as the final event in a long series of throws. But it is not at all likely that the system considered is ever totally chaotic. There always is a trace of order in it and it produces a bias favouring the slightly more frequent occurrence of certain die faces as final events. Analogous traces of order probably exist in all chaotic systems in this world. Similarly, one can be pretty certain that no system in this world is ever totally ordered. If it were, it would be a *perpetuum mobile*. There is always a lurking possibility of chaos and disorganization in the best of all ordered systems. Then the adjuvant circumstances of the system are no longer fully favourable to the occurrence of the usual chain of events.

In a totally ordered system, a causal chain may be pictured as stretched out in branching straight lines which never turn back on themselves. Yet such a picture is only plausible if the lines are thought of as extending along a purely temporal dimension. Moments of time advance in an undeviating progression from the past to the future. Time never flows backward. At least, this is accepted as a truism in our macroscopic world, though in the wonderland of subatomic physics a backward run of time has been occasionally considered as possible.

28

Reactive theories of disease

Branching causal chains may also be pictured as consisting of events which are given their location in three-dimensional space. Such chains would be lines that are far from straight, but twist in space in all directions. Take, for instance, the chain of events which begins with the stimulation of a spinal motoneurone and causes an action potential in its membrane; there follows the propagation of the action potential along the lengthy, winding, and eventually dividing course of the axon, the release of acetylcholine at the neuromuscular junctions, muscular action potentials, and finally the processes which contract the fibres in the muscular motor unit concerned.

These spatially extended causal chains can, of course, turn back on themselves, at least in certain branch lines. We then appear to have a causal chain that is a closed circuit. But it is a closed circuit in three-dimensional space only. In four-dimensional space-time, there is no closed circuit; there is instead a spiral extending along a temporal axis, because later events at the same spatial location are different from earlier events of the same kind. In ordered systems, such causal spirals (or 'circuits' as they are called in our customary three-dimensional phrasing) can have regulating functions, because they feed back information to spatial locations and thereby influence the events occurring there. Regulatory causal circuits are today known as 'feedback', or 'cybernetic' devices. They can be positive, co-ordinative, or negative.

Positive feedback regulations need checking devices to avoid runaway amplifications of the events in the causal circuit. For example, if we place a microphone too near to its loudspeaker, we have a positive feedback arrangement which is unchecked. Any sound picked up by the

29

microphone will come back to it through the loudspeaker, amplifying the sound already picked up. If this goes on unchecked there follows a runaway amplification of the sound into a loud howling whistle. In an ordered system, such as a living human body, positive feedback regulations are normally checked before runaway amplification can occur. Our skeletal muscles, for instance, have feedback devices in the form of sensory spindles. In certain circumstances, they give rise to a positive feedback circuit. This happens when their skeletal muscle is activated against a resistance that prevents contraction. In such 'isometric' activations, afferent impulses from the sensory spindles stimulate spinal motor cells which amplify the activation of the muscle concerned. Normally, this amplification is checked before painful cramps or muscle tears can occur.

Co-ordinating feedback centres for the regulation and refinement of the activities of skeletal muscles have their location in the central nervous system. They are modulated by messages from a variety of peripheral sense organs in muscles, tendons, joints, and skin. There are analogous co-ordinating feedback arrangements in the endocrine and immune systems of the body.

When it is a question of maintaining some steady state in a machine or in a living organism, negative feedback devices are commonly used. Thermostats and the 'governors' of steam engines are such devices which, respectively, bring about steady states of temperature and speed. In human bodies, there are comparable devices which maintain such steady states as body temperature, muscle tone, and various homeostatic levels. In a negative feedback circuit, an effect that is excessively large or excessively small brings about an inverse reaction in its causes. Too large an

30

effect lowers the power of its causes; too small an effect raises it. Excessive fluctuations of the effect are thus prevented and equilibria maintained. To give a homeostatic illustration: The thyroid-stimulating hormone (TSH) secreted by the anterior pituitary gland causes an increase in the level of thyroid hormones in the blood. If the increase is excessive, it brings about a reduction of TSH secretion. If this reduction lowers the level of thyroid hormones in the blood too much, the lowering causes an increase of TSH secretion. The blood level of thyroid hormones is thus maintained within narrow limits.

The various cybernetic regulations in a human body can be affected by pathological processes. As a result, positive feedbacks can give rise to too much amplification, coordinating feedback arrangements can be thrown out of gear, and negative feedback regulations can be set at abnormally high or low levels.

4

Source indicators and their perception

We have so far considered causal chains in a prospective direction, beginning with a cause and ending with a range of more or less probable effects. The task that confronts clinicians requires the tracing of causal chains in the opposite direction, beginning with clinical effects and unravelling retrospectively the causal chains leading to them. The task is intricate and difficult – so intricate and difficult that clinicians can hardly congratulate themselves on the degree of success they have achieved in general.

One of the difficulties of the clinical task is the fact that a combination of the same clinical effects can be the outcome of different kinds of causal chains in different patients. In other words, a particular combination of clinical manifestations is usually overdetermined in the sense that they can be the effects of independent causal chains converging on them.

There are fortunately occasional exceptions, when overdetermination is practically absent. An example is the disease of quartan malaria whose clinical description by Sydenham we have cited (p. 9). Indeed this is almost acceptable as indicating a monogenic disease entity whose causal chain within a patient's body has a particular pathological onset. If we add to Sydenham's description some additional clinical manifestations, such as the signs of haemolytic anaemia and of an enlarged spleen, we increase the likelihood of dealing with a monogenic disease entity

32

whose pathological onset was the arrival in the body of an environmental noxa in the form of protozoan micro-organisms belonging to the species *Plasmodium malariae*. Between the clinical picture and this pathological onset there must be a variety of intermediate pathological events. Some of them will be proximate to the clinical picture and more or less concomitant with it, and some of them will be of past occurrence and nearer to the pathological onset than the clinical picture.

Among the intermediate pathological events, proximate to and more or less concomitant with our clinical picture, is the presence in some erythrocytes of organisms of *Plasmodium malariae* in various stages of their asexual life cycle. Finding these organisms is of high diagnostic significance. It allows us to infer more distant intermediate events whose existence has been established by medical research in non-clinical settings, for example the past invasion of some liver cells by *Plasmodium malariae*. It also allows us to infer the past occurrence of the pathological onset of the monogenic disease entity of quartan malaria. We cannot, however, go further back in time without additional information about the manner of infection of the body by the environmental noxa. The usual manner of infection is through the bite of a female mosquito of the genus *Anopheles* in which organisms of *Plasmodium malariae* had gone through their sexual life cycles. Other less common modes of infection are through the injection of blood containing *Plasmodium malariae*, which may happen accidentally (e.g. through the unwitting trans-fusion of malarial blood or the use of contaminated syringes by drug addicts) and did at one time happen deliberately in the treatment of neurosyphilis. Another occasional mode of infection is through the passing of malaria-infected erythro-

33

cytes from the blood of a mother across the placenta to the blood of her embryo. Such different modes of infection all lead to the same kind of pathological onset, namely the arrival of *Plasmodium malariae* in the body of a patient. Earlier events take place in a spatio-temporal setting outside a patient's body and can be too diverse in kind to provide the required unitary and self-contained character of a mono- genic disease entity.

Most clinical pictures that were recognized in past ages did not have the same diagnostic penetration as the typical manifestations of quartan malaria. It was sheer chance that these manifestations turned out to belong to a monogenic disease entity. Indeed, it took centuries of clinical and extra-clinical research to prove that this was so, and pro- gress was often helped along by serendipity.

Even the clinical pictures which form diagnostic units today are usually not singular entities. They are overdeter- mined because we are still ignorant of the various patholog- ical onsets responsible in each case. Such causal ignorance is, of course, not peculiar to diagnostic clinical events; it is present with most other events and combinations of events.

There are, however, certain events which are, in normal circumstances and therefore almost always, uniquely determined; that is, they are end events on just one causal chain with its own source, its own initial cause. Such end events have a special role to play in science and technology. We shall call them *source indicators*. Their paradigm is the blue-litmus test. When it is positive, we can be practically certain that it is a source indicator of acidity in the fluid tested. In modern medicine, many source indicators are in use, but most of them reveal only intermediate pathological events. There are as yet few which reveal pathological

34

onsets. Those that do will be distinguished as *radical* source indicators. The presence of malaria parasites in the red-blood cells of a patient is such a radical source indicator.

Before any event can be accepted as a source indicator, certain conditions have to be met. Firstly, the source must not be just a conjectured event. It must be an event that is ascertainable by different source indicators. This is only possible when the event is also the source of different causal chains with different end events. An indicator whose source can thus be independently established is said to have *validity*. Without validity an event cannot be a source indicator. Secondly, a source indicator must, in normal circumstances, point to one particular kind of source only, and the normal circumstances should be so ubiquitous that we can usually rely on the source indicator. In that case, the source indicator is said to have a high degree of *reliability*. In abnormal circumstances, a source indicator may yield false positive or false negative results. The error can be detected because of the validity of the indicator which allows an independent ascertainment of the source. Thirdly, we want to know how efficient a source indicator is. When it responds sensitively to its source and reveals it in much detail, it will be said to have a high degree of *efficiency*. A positive blue-litmus test is valid, because the acidity of a fluid can be independently established. It is usually reliable, because it yields few false results. Its degree of efficiency is acceptable for many purposes, though it is lower than that of a pH meter reading.

In medicine, there has always been a tendency to promote events to the status of source indicators, long before their validity could possibly have been established. For instance, during the centuries when the theories of humoral

The concepts of illness, disease and morbus

pathology were in the ascendant, all clinical manifestations were believed to be source indicators of special abnormalities in bodily fluids. Yet such indications were no more than conjectures to which credibility was given by the dicta of authority and the general climate of medical opinion. The validity of the indicators could not be proved because there were none of the physical, chemical, and biological indicators of humoral abnormalities which are at our disposal today.

It was often easier for the physicians of past ages to establish the pathogenic role of certain external noxae than to clarify their pathological links with clinical manifestations. There are external noxae which can be objectively ascertained and whose pathogenic role is conspicuous, because they are fairly quickly and almost always followed by clinical consequences. Examples are physical assaults, heavy falls, poisonous snake bites, and so on. In these examples, the clinical consequences can be source indicators, because they are valid when the responsible noxa is independently identified, and because they are highly reliable, since the frequency and speed with which clinical consequences appear exclude other noxae. However, when such frequency and speed are lower, reliability may drop far enough to deprive clinical manifestations of their role of diagnostically acceptable source indicators, even when they validly point to a possible external noxa.

Ancient civilizations, for instance, knew that acute fevers are more frequent in communities near marshland than in those further away. They even had experimental proof of the existence of some marshland noxa, because land drainage reduced the incidence of acute fevers. Yet as we know today by hindsight, there are too many other causes of acute fevers to make these clinical events reliable indicators of a marshland source. In the past, the marshland source was presumed to be the bad air, the *mala aria*, in the misty and musty emanations of wet ground, and led to the diagnosis of malaria. When it was based merely on the clinical symptom of acute and recurrent fevers, it must often have been false because of their unreliability as source indicators. Today we make certain of our diagnosis by delaying it until malaria parasites have been found in erythrocytes. Such parasites must be the progeny of the first parasites that had entered the body of a patient. Their presence does not indicate a marshland noxa; it is a radical source indicator of a pathological onset which can be due to external noxae that have no direct connection with any marshland. Our radical source indicator of a malarial infection derives its validity from non-clinical experiments which have established the nature of the pathological onset. It derives its reliability from general biological laws which govern the ancestry of all living organisms. Because of these laws, its reliability is practically absolute.

It has to be realized that source indicators are not just events that occur in our environment. They must be events that are perceived; indeed not just perceived, but also recognized as source indicators. Such perceptions and recognitions are subjective experiences which can be communicated and thus made public.

All subjective experiences can be regarded as perceptions of which there are three general kinds: exteroceptions, introspections, and interoceptions. Some of these perceptions, but unfortunately not all of them, indicate their source in the form of events which can occur outside or inside our bodies. Those perceptions are thus *subjective*

37

source indicators. When the source in question is an event outside our bodies, it may be recognized as being itself a source indicator. We can thus distinguish subjective from *environmental* source indicators.

The subjective experiences which perceive events or objects outside our body or on its surface are *exteroceptions*. They function as subjective source indicators, when their validity and reliability can be demonstrated and their efficiency evaluated. Their validity and reliability are demonstrated when different people can exterocept the same environmental event and thus establish its veridical occurrence. Their efficiency depends on the amount of information they indicate.

There are several exteroceptive sensory systems at our disposal which provide us with different kinds of information about our environment. The most efficient among them is the exteroceptive visual system. Empirical scientific investigations therefore aim at basing themselves on visually exterocepted events. Exteroceptions involving gustatory and olfactory sensory systems are of only limited reliability and efficiency. Gustatory exteroceptions used to play a spurious diagnostic role in medicine in past centuries, when doctors were in the habit of tasting a patient's urine. There is no place for them in modern medicine, and there is only a minor place for olfactory exteroceptions, such as the observation that the breath of a comatose patient has the fruity-sweet smell of acetone which indicates the acidosis of a severe disease of diabetes mellitus. Tactile, thermal, and auditory exteroceptions still have their definite diagnostic uses in initial clinical examinations. Yet the general trend in the clinical diagnostics of today is towards the use of visual exteroceptions and the discovery of ever more methods of investigation which will provide us with visual source indicators of events within the body of patients. Among those methods are surgical procedures, endoscopic, radiographic and similar devices, as well as a host of visually assessed laboratory tests.

The second kind of perception available to us is that of *introspection*. It consists of conscious experiences of cognitive and emotional phenomena as well as of mental drives which can be impulsive, compulsive, or deliberate. Introspections are unfortunately no source indicators at all. We only know that their sources must be events which occur in the brain somewhere and somehow. About the nature of these events we are still in utter ignorance, so ignorant indeed that we can do no better than choose between the contradictory speculations that have been elaborated by different metaphysical schools of thought.

There are dualistic schools of thought which believe that introspected experiences have their source in events which occur in a mental substance and that these events are essentially different from the physical events in material substances. Such dualistic views have their modern origin in the doctrines of Descartes who expounded them in the seventeenth century. Yet he and all other dualists have not been able to explain satisfactorily how two such disparate kinds of events as those of the body and those of the mind co-exist and interact.

The alternatives to dualistic views are monistic ones. According to them, there can be only one kind of event in this world and it must be either physical or mental. In modern science and medicine, monistic views of a physicalistic kind prevail. In that case, introspected experiences have their source in physical events in the brain. They are double-aspect events, since they present themselves in introspected form to the person in whose brain they occur; yet, since they are physical events, they should in principle be also exteroceptible in some ways, at least by indirect means, through suitable environmental source indicators. But such source indicators do not yet exist. Only in science-fiction terms might we imagine some esoteric cerebroscope yielding exteroceptible data which reveal the physical events in the brain of the person who introspects them. This double-aspect view of the cerebral sources of introspection has led to physicalistic theories of mind–body identity (Armstrong, 1968; O'Connor, 1969).

Some of the source events that are introspectively experienced by a person also have consequences in his body which can be noticed by him and by others through non-introspective channels. In particular, when those consequences consist in overt behaviour, including verbal communications, they can be exterocepted by other people. Such exteroceptible overt behaviour must not be viewed as a source indicator of introspected experiences. They are neither valid nor reliable. They are not valid, because there are no independent source indicators of privately introspected phenomena. They are not reliable, because they may have an unconscious origin which cannot be introspected, and even if they have an introspected origin, this need not accord with the exteroceptible overt behaviour which may be deceptive and is liable to misinterpretation.

The third kind of perception at our disposal is the *interoceptive* one. It consists of consciously experienced sensations whose sources are events within our bodies excluding the brain. The sensations can be differentiated into proprioceptive and nociceptive ones.

Source indicators and their perception

Some *proprioceptive* sensations provide a person with information about raised pressures in his bladder, rectum, and voluntary muscles. The sensations indicate their bodily sources reliably and efficiently in normal circumstances. It has also been established that they do so validly. They are thus subjective source indicators. Other proprioceptive sensations make a person aware of the positions and movements of his body in a gravitational field, and of the relative positions of his trunk, extremities and head. The validity, reliability and efficiency of these sensations in normal circumstances can be readily established through the exteroception of their source by independent observers. They are thus also subjective source indicators. This is not surprising, since they obviously have great survival value. Indeed their efficiency can be raised through practice and training to an impressive degree of manual, acrobatic, and balancing skill.

Nociceptive sensations are experienced in the form of aches, pains, and other discomforts. Such experiences are, of course, frequent among the complaints of patients. They are, for most people, abnormal experiences whose sources are abnormal events within a patient's body, events which are usually pathological, except when they occur in the course of a normal pregnancy, during labour or during penitential religious exercises. But nociceptive sensations need not validly indicate the location of their bodily sources or convey any information about their nature. Examples are the referred pains of damaged visceral organs or nerve roots, or the feelings of nausea due to pregnancy or lesions in the brain or inner ear. Nociceptive sensations are thus often not source indicators at all and may be totally unreliable in their subjective localizations. It is then the task of

41

clinicians to clarify their origin, if possible with the help of environmental source indicators.

The complaints which are conveyed to the clinicians are not always just nociceptive interoceptions experienced by the patient himself. They also consist of other observations made by the patient and/or his social environment which have given rise to concern about his health. All such complaints are known as clinical *symptoms*. They are often poor and deceptive source indicators of their pathological background so that their diagnostic value can be of a low order. For this reason, clinicians have always tried to supplement clinical symptoms by enquiries and investigations which require medical experience, expertise, and today often the use of intricate instruments and sophisticated apparatus. The observations which a clinician can thus add to a patient's symptoms are known as clinical *signs*. Clinicians endow them with diagnostic value, but this does not necessarily mean that clinical signs are source indicators of pathological changes or even radical source indicators of pathological onsets. To convert clinical signs into source indicators of diagnostic value the nature of the source and its causal significance has to be established by research which usually has to be carried out in non-clinical settings.

As long as such research has not yielded positive results, a clinical sign may merely have some prognostic value and perhaps suggest some therapeutic regime, even if that has only a placebo effect. As an illustration, let us have a look at a clinical sign which was known to Indian physicians at least as early as the third century B.C. It was the sign of a sweet-tasting urine and was mentioned in a medico-surgical compilation of that time, known as the 'Sushruta Samhitá' (Vol. II, p. 46). The sign remained common medical knowledge throughout the centuries. In the seventeenth century, Thomas Willis noticed that it was associated in most patients with a special triad of clinical symptoms consisting of polydipsia, polyuria, and emaciation. The triad had been familiar already to early Greek physicians who regarded it as indicating a disease they called 'diabetes' from a Greek word for syphon, because the patients functioned like syphons, taking in fluid at one end and discharging it at the other.

Eventually it was found that urine tasted sweet when it contained glucose. The clinical sign was therefore called 'glycosuria'. Chemical tests of glycosuria were developed whose results were visually exteroceptible. Doctors were thus freed from the disagreeable and unreliable gustatory exteroception of glycosuria. Clinicians then noticed that glycosuria could be present long before the diabetic triad of symptoms made its appearance in a patient. The result was that the sign of glycosuria was accepted as an early indicator of the disease of diabetes. But this did not mean that the sign of glycosuria had become a source indicator of pathological events. Those events still remained unknown.

What were these events? A possible answer was given by Claude Bernard in the 1850s. His non-clinical experiments suggested that glycosuria was a source indicator of hyperglycaemia. As a source indicator it had validity, because the presence of hyperglycaemia could be independently established by laboratory tests. It was, however, not fully reliable, as was eventually found, because glycosuria was not always due to hyperglycaemia. It could be due to a diminished glucose reabsorption in renal tubules, a harmless abnormality that was originally termed 'renal diabetes'. It was also noticed in due course that two components of the diabetic triad, namely polydipsia and polyuria, could be present without glycosuria or hyperglycaemia. This was a rare clinical condition which obliged clinicians to distinguish between diabetes mellitus and diabetes insipidus.

Positive laboratory tests of hyperglycaemia are clinical signs which are valid and reliable source indicators of hyperglycaemia in a patient. But hyperglycaemia in a patient is an overdetermined event. It does not always have its origin in the disease of diabetes mellitus. The diagnostically decisive clinical sign of the disease of diabetes mellitus is not just a positive laboratory test of hyperglycaemia, but tests must show an abnormally high and prolonged hyperglycaemic response to a glucose tolerance test. For a time, it seemed that such an abnormal glucose tolerance test was a source indicator of a Virchowian disease entity which consisted in damage to the beta cells of the Langerhans islets of the pancreas and a consequent reduction of insulin secretion. That damage seemed to be the pathological basis of diabetes mellitus and some allied diseases. It was indeed present in some patients with diabetes mellitus and always in such allied diseases as haemochromatosis ('bronze diabetes'), chronic pancreatitis, or pancreatectomy. Yet patients with these allied diseases are more amenable to insulin treatment than many patients with diabetes mellitus in whom there is a reduction of insulin efficiency rather than of insulin secretion. Diabetes mellitus due to such a reduction of insulin efficiency is not a monogenic disease entity, since it seems to derive from different pathological onsets which have, however, not yet been clearly identified. There is some evidence that some pathological onsets may consist in diabetogenic genes in the zygote. Yet such genes need not be pathogenic by themselves; they may only be responsible for a diabetic predisposition. This turns into an overt disease, when there are adverse adjuvant circumstances such as dietetic habits which are selective noxae.

When research has not yet uncovered a pathological chain of events in its full length from its pathological onset to its clinical manifestations, doctors have to resort to methods of classification to bring order into the data available to them. They are sustained in their classifying efforts by the hope that whatever order they can establish will indicate causal origins and thus show the way to the detection of Virchowian and perhaps even monogenic disease entities. Let us therefore now turn to an examination of the advantages and limitations of classifications.

5

Classes and classifications

We can distinguish two kinds of classes: a) empirical classes composed of concrete entities and b) theoretical or non-empirical classes composed of abstract entities. Logicians deal schematically with both kinds of classes and especially with the relationships that exist between classes, on the one hand, and between classes and any sub-classes or entities within them, on the other.

We shall begin with the consideration of a particular empirical class, namely the class of human beings. Let us, first of all, note that the expression 'the class of human beings' consists of two components. The first component is a singular noun, 'class'. This is a collective noun which conceptually unifies a plurality of entities in our example. Like other collective nouns, it can be used in the singular or plural. Take, for instance, the collective noun 'committee'. We can say that a committee *has* agreed, or *have* agreed, on a particular decision. Both formulations are grammatically correct, but the plural formulation makes more sense, because it takes two or more individuals to agree on some-thing.

The term 'class', being a collective noun, thus has two aspects. It can signify a conceptual unification of a plurality and thus designate a class entity, or unity, something that Bertrand Russell had once called 'the class as one' (1937, p. 76; first edition, 1903). The term can also denote all and every entity in a plurality, something which was for

Classes and classifications

Bertrand Russell at one time 'the class as many' (Russell, 1937).

The second component in the expression 'the class of human beings' is the plural of the term 'human being'. This is a 'general' term which can be applied separately to every concrete entity in our empirical class. The entities in our class thus share that general name, but are differentiated by their 'personal', or 'proper', names.

The entities which collectively form a class are known in logical terminology as the *extension* of the class (though the term can have other meanings as well). Not all extensions consist of many entities. If an extension consists of only one entity, its class is a unit class. An example is the class of terrestrial moons. If an extension consists of no entities at all, its class is the null, or empty, class. Examples are the empirical class of Greek Gods and the non-empirical class of square circles.

A particular entity can be in the extension of several classes. A particular person, for instance, may be in the extension of such classes as his family, neighbourhood, country, mankind, and so on. The relation between an entity and any of its classes is a very special one. In logical terminology, it is called 'the relation of *membership*', or 'the relation of *belonging*'. It is a curious and interesting fact that this relation had been largely overlooked or only inadequately grasped in the traditional logic of former times. Its significance was clearly established for the first time by the German philosopher and mathematician, Gottlob Frege, in 1879. It is also historically curious and interesting that Frege's important contributions to the field of logic and mathematics remained unknown and unacknowledged for decades, especially in his native country. In a German

47

The concepts of illness, disease and morbus

Philosophen-Lexicon (ed. W. Ziegenfuss) of 1949, his name was not even mentioned. He fared much better in the English-speaking world. This was due in the beginning to Bertrand Russell who said of Frege in his *History of Western Philosophy* (1961, p. 784): 'In spite of the epoch-making nature of his discoveries, he remained wholly without recognition until I drew attention to him in 1903'. The subsequent neglect of Frege in Germany may have been associated with the exodus of many German philosophers during the Hitler régime. This at least is the opinion of Christian Thiel (1972, p. 11) who remarked: 'It is not surprising that Frege became known in the first place abroad in English-speaking countries through German philosophers who in those twelve years had left Germany mostly against their will'.

The logical systems of former times had dealt inadequately, if at all, with the relation of membership that obtains between an individual entity and its class. It had concentrated on a different relation, namely that which obtains between a sub-class and its class. A sub-class, considered as a plurality, does not have a membership relation to its class; it has a special relation which logicians have come to call *'inclusion'*, or *'containment'*. The relation of inclusion, however, has totally different characteristics from those of the relation of membership. That this is so has become fully clear only since Frege's contribution to logical theory. The most important of these differences concerns the attribute of transitivity. This is an attribute with which we are familiar from the algebra of equality. For example, if $a = b$ and $b = c$, then $a = c$. Similarly, if a sub-class is (are) included (or contained) in a class and the latter is (are) included in a super-class, then the sub-class is (are) also included in the super-class. For example, the sub-class of medical men is (are) included in the class of professional men, and the latter is (are) included in the class of university graduates, therefore the sub-class of medical men is (are) also included in the class of university graduates. In general parlance, we hardly ever use the terms 'class' or 'include' in this context. Instead we just mention the class members, but not the class, and link them with the help of the grammatical copula 'are'. Medical men are professional men, professional men are university graduates, therefore medical men are university graduates. This kind of reasoning is a logical syllogism of the kind which was first examined in detail by Aristotle.

But the membership relation is not transitive. An entity is a member of a class (considered as a plurality), that class (considered as an entity) is a member of a class of classes, yet the original entity is not a member of the class of classes. Dr So-and-so is a member of the profession of medical men (a plurality), the medical profession (an entity) is a member of the class of professions (a plurality), yet Dr So-and-so is not a member of the class of professions. In general parlance, we do not usually talk of 'being a member of a class'. Instead we use the grammatical copula 'is' which links an entity as a subject with a general term as a predicate. Our reasoning then becomes: Dr So-and-so is a medical man, the medical profession is a professional class, but Dr So-and-so is not a professional class.

The membership of a class can be described in two ways. One way consists in listing all the members separately, if there are any. This is known as the 'extensional' approach. It is available in principle rather than in practice, since many classes are too large to make this approach feasible. However, we can use this approach to provide an illustration.

The concepts of illness, disease and morbus

For example, let us consider the class consisting of the two children (Peter and Paul) of a family K. Adopting the customary notation of modern set theory, we simply put down the names of the two children, separate them by a comma, and enclose them in a pair of braces. The result is

$$\{Peter, Paul\} \qquad (1)$$

The alternative to this extensional approach consists in listing the special attributes (properties, qualities, characteristics) which distinguish our class from all other classes. Here we have only one special attribute. In set notation, it would look like this:

$$\{x: x \text{ is a child of family } K\} \qquad (2)$$

and this can be read as 'the class of all the entities x such that every x is a child of family K'.

W. and M. Kneale, in their review of *The Development of Logic* (1964, p. 318), state that the differentiation between the two approaches to the description of the members of a particular class was 'the best remembered contributions of the *Port Royal Logic*' of seventeenth century France. Its two authors, A. Arnauld and P. Nicole, had distinguished between the 'comprehension' and the 'extension' of a general class concept (or a general class term). To quote from W. & M. Kneale: 'The comprehension of a general term, then, is the set of attributes which it implies. . . . The extension of a term, on the other hand, is the set of things to which it is applicable. . . . Since *compréhension* means in ordinary French the same as "understanding" does in English, it is natural to assume that Arnauld and Nicole intend to refer here to what we understand by a term, i.e. its *significatum* or meaning. But their definition and example do not support

Classes and classifications

this view. . . . Since the middle of the nineteenth century English writers have commonly followed Sir William Hamilton [1860] in replacing "comprehension" by "intension", which has no use in ordinary language.'

We can therefore say that a class can be described extensionally or intensionally. Expression (2) above is an example of an intensional description. It is often the only one available to us.

The term 'intension' has in due course acquired additional meanings in logical literature, but we shall use it here in its original meaning as denoting the set of attributes which is the necessary and sufficient condition for membership in a particular class and therefore distinguishes the members of that class from the members of other classes. We shall later address ourselves particularly to an examination of the intension which characterizes the members of the universal class of all patients and to an examination of the intensions of certain particular classes of patients. A universal class of whatever entities is also known as a 'domain', or 'universe of discourse', when no entities outside that class are considered.

When logicians consider the characteristics and relationships of classes, they have highly schematized classes in mind which differ from the classes with which empirical scientists deal in their actual investigations and their theoretical evaluations. Yet this difference has not received sufficient recognition from logicians in spite of its practical importance.

In this context, the considerations of logicians are governed by one of their most fundamental axioms known as 'the axiom of non-contradiction'. It stipulates that an entity cannot be both a member and a non-member of a particular

The concepts of illness, disease and morbus

class. The axiom has very convenient consequences. It follows from it that classes must be exactly demarcated by sharp boundaries, that they are *exact* classes. This exactness presupposes that all the members of a class are completely equal in their class-distinctive characteristics, that they exhibit the various attributes in their class intension in their totality and to the same degree.

The sharp demarcation of exact classes makes it possible to divide each of them into two complementary sub-classes whose members are mutually exclusive and jointly exhaustive. This means that every member of an exact class must belong to one, and only one, of the two complementary sub-classes and that there are no class members which do not belong to one of the two complementary sub-classes.

The empirical classes with which scientists deal in their practical investigations are different from the highly schematized classes of logicians. Stephan Körner (1966) has taken account of this difference. He pointed out (pp. 23ff) that the members of an empirical class are usually not equal in their class-distinctive characteristics. They are only similar in this respect as they do not have to exhibit all the attributes listed in their class intension, and those they exhibit can vary in degree. Empirical classes are thus usually 'resemblance' classes. Yet resemblances can wear thinner and thinner, until we are eventually left to doubt whether certain entities still belong to the empirical class examined. When this happens, empirical classes are vaguely demarcated. They are then not only resemblance classes, they are also *inexact* classes.

It follows that reasoning which is applicable to the schematized classes of logic can be used with reservations only, when empirical classes are under consideration. With inexact classes, the axiom of non-contradiction holds no longer. We cannot any more say that an entity is either a member or a non-member of an inexact class. The entity in question may be a borderline candidate which may be regarded with equal justification as a member or a non-member. Take, for instance, the inexact class of all green objects. The intension of this class consists of all the shades of green in the spectrum which merge gradually into yellow or blue with diminishing green tinges. There is no definite boundary anywhere so that membership in this class will be a problematic borderline for many objects.

However, empirical classes need not be inexact at all times. Sharp natural boundaries may develop in certain empirical classes and arbitrary boundaries may be imposed for practical purposes in certain empirical or non-empirical classes.

The most notable example of sharp natural boundaries, evolving in the course of time, is to be found in those empirical classes which constitute established biological species. An established biological species is an exact class, because all its members are equal in one respect: they are all unable to interbreed successfully with the members of other biological species. This criterion of 'reproductive isolation' is the hallmark of an established species and is responsible for making the species an exact class. Of course, in the early stages of an evolving species, the boundaries cannot have been exact; there must have been borderline members that, in principle at least, were capable of interbreeding success-fully with members both of the original species and of the newly evolving one, provided there were no geographical or other impediments to such interbreeding. But by the time a particular species has become fully established, there are no borderline members any more. There is no longer any possibility of successful interbreeding with such closely related species as, for example, the African and Indian elephant or the Arabian and Bactrian camel. Once two closely related species have established themselves, their respective gene pools will undergo independent changes and bring about structural and functional characteristics which differentiate the two species.

Whereas the members of an established species are equal with regard to the characteristic of reproductive isolation which is present in every species, they are only similar with regard to those characteristics by which different species are distinguished. The latter characteristics show variations due to such influences as age, sex, accident, disease, race, variety, strain, and the like. Yet such variations do not lead to borderline members, unless a new species is about to evolve. In all other circumstances, the intension of an established species is distinctive and is sharply differentiated from the intensions of other species.

Such exact demarcations and sharp differentiations through the workings of the natural phenomenon of reproductive isolation occurs, however, only among biological species. At any higher level in the hierarchy of biological classes, there are no natural phenomena, comparable to reproductive isolation, which could give rise to exact demarcations. At such higher levels, arbitrary decisions have had to be made to ensure exact demarcations of an artificial kind.

It is the task of taxonomists, or systematists, to bring order into the biological domain through adequate classifications. The biological domain may be viewed as an empirical domain. In that case, its basic entities are biological organisms. It is, however, usually viewed as a theoretical domain whose basic entities are biological species considered as class entities. For taxonomists, a species is a *taxon* of the lowest level. They describe taxa intensionally by establishing the set of attributes that distinguishes the members of a taxon from the members of all other taxa at the same level in the classificatory hierarchy. In the language of modern taxonomists that set of attributes, i.e. the intension of a taxon, is called an 'operational taxonomic unit, or OTU'. Taxa above the level of species are in ascending direction genera, orders, families, classes, phyla, and the three kingdoms of plants, animals, and protista.

The early taxonomists had confidently assumed that higher-level taxa will turn out to be exact classes so that all the species in them would have taxon-distinctive sets of attributes in their intensions and thus be sharply demarcated from the species in other higher taxa at the same level in the classificatory hierarchy. Unfortunately, this assumption has proved untenable in the face of practical difficulties. As Sokal & Sneath (1963) remarked: 'Every systematist knows of instances where a character previously considered to be diagnostic of a taxon is lacking in a newly discovered organism [i.e. species] which clearly belongs to the taxon'. For example, there are birds without wings, vertebrates without red blood, and mammals which do not bear their offspring. There are thus members of the domain of biological species that may with almost equal justification be regarded as belonging to one or the other of two higher-level taxa which should be mutually exclusive in their membership.

Consider, for instance, the zoological class of mammals. It is a higher-level taxon and includes several mammalian orders, such as the order of primates, carnivores, rodents, and so on. The mammalian intension contains such taxon-distinctive attributes as bearing live young, feeding them with milk from mammary teats, being warm-blooded, having single jawbones, characteristically differentiated teeth, and the like. All mammalian species should exhibit these class-distinctive attributes *in toto*. Most of them do. But there are exceptions. They concern species in the zoological order of monotremes, such as the species of the duck-billed platypus and the spiny ant-eater. This zoological order has in its intension a mixture of some distinctive mammalian and some equally distinctive reptilian attributes. Taxonomists wavered for a while in their opinions as to whether to include the order of monotremes in the class of mammals or in the class of reptiles. However, in the end agreement was reached that the order of monotremes should be included among the mammals.

The result has been to make the class of mammalian species artificially exact, but at the cost of waiving the principle that all mammalian species should exhibit the distinctive mammalian attributes *in toto*. Similar difficulties in achieving clean-cut classifications have been encountered with other high-level biological taxa. Taxonomists have had no choice but to lower their ambitions. They have agreed to distinguish two kinds of taxa. The first kind has just one list of taxon-distinctive attributes in their intensions. Such taxa have been called 'monothetic' (i.e. single-list). They are exact resemblance classes without borderline members. All their members exhibit *all* the taxon-distinctive attributes but not to the same degree. The second kind of taxa have intensions compounded of several overlapping lists of attributes. They have been called 'polythetic' (Sneath, 1962). The rule in them is that species members need exhibit only 'a large proportion' of the attributes in the intensions. Polythetic taxa are also exact resemblance classes.

After this initiation into the characteristics of classes and their relationships, let us now turn to one of our main tasks: the division of the domain of human beings into two complementary classes of patients and non-patients. Since the domain of human beings is an empirical class, a division of it into two complementary classes yields two empirical classes, i.e. classes whose members are concrete individuals. We could establish such classes in an 'ostensive' manner as suggested by Körner (1966, pp. 24ff), for instance.

We begin with two special groups of human beings. The members of one of these groups are 'standard' patients and the members of the other group 'standard' non-patients. In other words, one group contains human beings who are undoubtedly ill and the other group human beings who are undoubtedly healthy. Having thus obtained two cores of standard patients and standard non-patients respectively, we can now add all the other human beings in the domain to either of the two cores according to whether they are 'in a certain respect and to a certain degree' similar to standard patients but not also to standard non-patients. We thus obtain a class of largely 'ordinary' patients and a class of largely 'ordinary' non-patients. There will, however, remain a 'neutral', or 'borderline', group of people who 'in a certain respect and to a certain degree' are similar to both ordinary patients and ordinary non-patients. They could thus be assigned with equal justification to the class of patients or the class of non-patients. We cannot be surprised about this state of affairs, since we are dealing with empirical classes of inexact demarcation. As long as we remain undecided about the assignment of borderline candidates, the empirical classes of patients and non-patients cannot be complementary because, though they are mutually exclusive, they are not exhaustive with regard to the domain of human beings, since they leave borderline candidates out of account. If we want to remove this impasse, we have to take quite arbitrary decisions. We may, for instance, decide to put all the borderline candidates into the class of patients. In doing so, we would follow the example set by taxonomists. As a result, we shall expect our class of patients to be a polythetic resemblance class that has been made arbitrarily exact in its demarcation. The same result would have been obtained, if we had assigned all the borderline candidates to the class of non-patients.

Ostensive procedures of the kind described have often been amiss, when they took account only of superficial characteristics which are readily demonstrable. The results could therefore turn out to have been misleading. For example, whales were once included in the class of fishes (they are even called 'Walfische' in German), because the intension of that class contained then as an essential component the attribute of living exclusively in water. Similarly, bats were once included in the class of birds, because the intension of that class contained then as an essential component the attribute of flying. Closer investigations eventually changed the intensions of both these classes and therefore the definition of membership in them. Membership in the class of fishes became defined by the essential attributes of living exclusively in water, breathing through gills and having limbs which take the form of fins. This new definition excluded whales from the class of fishes. Similarly, membership in the class of birds became defined by the essential attribute of being feathered bipeds. This new definition excluded bats from the class of birds, because bats are featherless bipeds (and in this respect like human beings).

The establishment of a particular class in a domain thus requires close attention to the task of finding the most important attributes to be put into its intension. This is the task that confronts us in establishing the universal class of all patients.

Before approaching this task, we have to clarify the relation between the intension as a whole and the attributes composing it. The intension as a whole is a compound attribute. We can talk about it even without knowing the composing attributes in detail. But we may need a name by which to designate it, an abstract name. Such names are usually fashioned from the general name of the class members by adding a suffix like '-hood', '-ity', or '-ness'. The general name in our class is 'patient'. Our abstract name might therefore be 'patienthood'. However, this has an awkward ring. To avoid this, let us form our abstract name from the adjectival general term 'morbid', since the class of patients and of morbid beings can be regarded as identical through having the same members. We thus obtain the abstract name 'morbidity'. It is a familiar name in medicine as it is commonly used to designate the prevalence of diseases in a community. In the present context, it will designate the compound attribute in the intension of the universal class of all patients.

Our task may now be seen as aiming at the semantic clarification of the concept of morbidity in general and of the various forms of morbidity which define membership in particular classes of patients.

are featherless bipeds (and in this respect like human
beings).

The establishment of a particular class in a domain thus

6

Morbidity

The problem we wish to tackle in this chapter concerns the
clarification of the concept of morbidity in general. So far,
we have presented the concept merely globally as a set of
attributes, a compound characteristic, which constitutes the
intension of the universal class of all patients. To clarify
this global concept we have to consider what attributes
best characterize it. The attributes must be such that
they provide a satisfactory, even if not definitive, elucid-
ation of the concept which, at this stage in our presentation,
is so hazy as to have hardly any discernible semantic
content.

It is widely assumed that the attributes in question must,
singly or in combination, differ significantly from a norm
and must thus be abnormal. Sometimes that norm is viewed
in high-minded perfectionistic terms. A person who is
healthy according to this view can have only attributes
which are perfect. There can be no blemish of any sort in
him. In other words, the concept of health would be entirely
composed of ideally perfect attributes. The World Health
Organization has lent its prestige to such a view by asserting
that 'health is a state of complete physical, mental and social
well-being'. This perfectionistic view of health is, of course,
of no practical help. Ideal norms are by definition unattain-
able in our imperfect world. To adopt them has the inevitable result of denouncing all human beings as substandard

physically, mentally, and socially. Indeed it would make abnormality a universal attribute not only of mankind, but of all biological organisms.

To be practically useful the concept of abnormality must be approached from a statistical angle. From this viewpoint, abnormality is a characteristic of those attributes which occur in only a minority of the members of a domain. Attributes are thus abnormal in a domain, if they are unusual in it.

In the context of morbidity, the domain that is generally taken into account is the empirical domain of biological organisms or merely the empirical domain of human beings. However, this is not the only domain that has to be considered here. There is another domain which must be examined. It is a chronological domain whose members are not concrete individuals but days or other time spans in an individual's life.

Let us look at the domain of human beings first. Since it is impossible in practice to examine the whole of that domain because it is far too vast, statisticians are content with the investigation of samples of human beings, provided those samples are unbiased and representative. It is customary to regard attributes, or values of attributes, as statistically normal when they occur in at least 95% of the members of such a sample. Applying this criterion, we can say that the attribute of having two eyes is statistically normal in the human domain and so are the values of body temperature which lie within the normal range, i.e. within the norm that extends from 36 °C to 37 °C. Having fewer than two eyes or being hyperthermic or hypothermic are abnormal human attributes.

Unfortunately, the ascertainment of statistical norms and

61

statistical abnormalities is not always quite as straightforward. There often are practical difficulties. In many contexts, we cannot use samples which are representative of the whole domain of human beings. If we did, we would run the risk of obtaining false impressions of the norms of certain attributes or attribute values. The reason is that the human domain is stratified. It contains natural subdivisions in which some attributes have norms of their own. Consider, for instance, the attribute of excretory continence. It is the norm in the class of adult human beings. It is certainly not the norm in the class of human babies.

Excretory continence belongs to the group of attributes which are assessed as either present or absent, which can, as it were, have only the two values of presence and absence. There is another group of attributes which are present in all human beings but to a varying degree. Such attributes have many different values when assessed on some scale of measurement. The norm of such attributes is not their average value as is sometimes erroneously believed; it is a range of values such as we have already seen in the case of body temperature. Yet that range of normal values can be significantly different in certain natural subdivisions of the human domain. Let us take the attribute of body weight as an example. In a representative sample of the whole human domain, the range of normal values of body weight is bound to extend too far towards the lower end of the scale. How far will depend on a variety of factors, especially on the proportion of children and young people in the sample. There are quite a few natural sub-classes of human beings with norms of body weight of their own. To find such classes we can use as criteria any attributes which correlate with body weight. Age is one such criterion, as we have already indicated. Sex, height, ethnic origin, and even fashions of beauty and ideas of prestige are others. The proportion of such sub-classes in a sample of human beings can introduce a bias which distorts the normal range of body weight values.

Attribute norms which are established in samples of human beings will be termed *population norms,* or *population standards* (cf. Taylor, 1966, p. 4), using the term 'population' in its etymologically original sense as referring to *populi*, people.

When we turn to the chronological domain whose members are days or other time spans in the life of an individual person, we may find that most of his attributes during a recent past have remained more or less constant. If that is so, we shall say that those attributes exhibit his *individual norm,* or *individual standard*.

We can expect that most of the attributes of a healthy person are normal by both population standards and his individual standards. In a person who has fallen ill recently some attributes will be abnormal by both population and his individual standards. It is, however, possible that there is no such concordance for certain attributes in a person who has fallen ill recently. A previously obese person, for instance, might lose so much weight that the value of this attribute now falls within the normal population range, though it is, of course, now abnormal by his individual norm. A chronic patient, on the other hand, has some attributes which are abnormal by population norms and yet normal by his individual norms.

If we take both population and individual norms into account, we may say that patients are characterized by certain attributes which are statistically abnormal by one and/or both kinds of norm. Yet this does not mean that an

abnormality of attributes has a diagnostic medical significance by itself. It has not. There are many statistically
abnormal attributes which have no diagnostic medical significance whatsoever. On the contrary, they can be social
assets. Examples are abnormally high values (by population
standards) of intelligence, attractiveness, creative ability,
manual skill or abnormally high values (by individual standards) of achievement after a period of study, training, or
exercise.

If we postulate, as we well may, that the majority of
human beings do not, at any one time, belong to the universal class of patients, then it follows that morbidity in general
is a compound attribute that is statistically abnormal by
population and/or individual norms. The same can also be
said of the various particular forms of morbidity which are
called by such general names as 'disease', 'illness', 'disorder', 'sickness', 'ailment', and the like. It is necessary to
consider always both the population standard and the individual standards of an attribute. If only one standard is
considered, then it is possible that some of the attributes of a
particular form of morbidity are normal by that standard.
We have already mentioned that the body weight of an
obese person can, through some intervening disease processes, become normal by population standards. Yet his
body weight would then be abnormal by his individual
standard for that attribute.

It therefore seems justified to assume that all the attributes which compose morbidity in general or any particular
form of morbidity will be found to be abnormal by at least
one of the two statistical standards we have considered. If
we call the attributes which compose morbidity, whether
general or particular, by the name 'morbid', then we can

state that all morbid attributes are abnormal. But it is obvious that the converse is not the case. Only some abnormal attributes are also morbid. In other words, the theoretical sub-class of morbid attributes is included in the larger theoretical class of abnormal attributes.

The consideration of abnormality has thus been of only limited help in our task of clarifying the concept of morbidity. We are still left with the problem of finding the criteria which distinguish morbid attributes from merely abnormal ones.

It is rather surprising how rarely this problem has attracted the attention of medical men. The explanation may lie in the difficulty of working out a generally acceptable solution. In any case few solutions have been suggested. One such solution came from Scadding (1967). He stated: 'A disease is the sum of the abnormal phenomena displayed by a group of living organisms in association with a specific common characteristic or set of characteristics by which they differ from the norm for their species in such a way as to place them at a biological disadvantage'.

This statement is about a disease, i.e. a particular form of morbidity. It asserts in effect that a disease is composed of attributes (phenomena) which are not only abnormal by their population (species) norm, but also place the living organisms displaying the disease at a biological disadvantage.

Scadding talks only of abnormalities by population standards. He does not consider the role individual standards play in establishing the abnormality of attributes. This, however, is only a minor point of criticism. What deserves our main attention is his important suggestion that morbid attributes are different from merely abnormal ones by being associated with biological disadvantage.

The concepts of illness, disease and morbus

Before examining this suggestion, let us, first of all, enlarge its scope. This is certainly justified for, when Scadding talks of 'a disease' what he obviously has in mind is 'any disease' or 'all diseases'. Particular diseases are distinguished by their own special set of morbid attributes. But there must also be a set of morbid attributes that characterizes all diseases. Such a set of morbid attributes would constitute the intension of the theoretical class of all diseases, an intension which we have called 'morbidity in general' and distinguished from particular forms of morbidity, such as particular diseases. In Scadding's sense, morbidity in general would also be composed of attributes that are abnormal by population standards and are associated with biological disadvantage.

Scadding did not attempt to clarify the concept of biological disadvantage, though he was well aware that such clarification was needed. He remarked that 'the rather vague term "biological disadvantage" is as precise a statement (*sic*) as can be made about the criteria on which it is generally decided whether their deviation from a norm is to be regarded as associated with disease or not'. He left it at that. But can a vague concept reduce the vagueness of a concept it is supposed to clarify?

Recently, Kendell (1975a) has sought to dispel some of the vagueness of the concept of biological disadvantage. He said: 'Scadding avoided elaborating on what he meant by "biological disadvantage". Presumably, though, it must embrace both increased mortality and reduced fertility' (p. 310). Combining this with Scadding's proposition that abnormal attributes with biological disadvantage are necessary components of any disease, Kendell came to some unusual conclusions. He stated, for instance: 'My interpre-

66

tation of "biological disadvantage" – *restricting it to conditions which reduce fertility and shorten life* – means that some conditions, like post-herpetic neuralgia and psoriasis, fail to qualify as illnesses despite the fact that they cause considerable suffering, are accompanied by well-defined lesions, and are capable of being relieved by medical means' (p. 310, my italics).

Kendell considered the question of whether biological disadvantage should be judged from the point of view of the individual or the species. He came down unreservedly in favour of the individual. 'For a characteristic to qualify as a biological disadvantage it must be shown to be harmful to the individual possessing it, and also to be innate and not simply one that leads to rejection by others' (p. 314). This view does not accord well, however, with some arguments by Kendell which imply that reduced fertility by itself can be the hallmark of biological disadvantage. He mentions homosexuals and transsexuals (p. 311) in this respect and might as well have added people who adopt a devotional life of chastity or use birth-control measures.

The awkwardness of Kendell's conclusions highlights Scadding's wisdom in refraining from the job of clarifying the concept of biological disadvantage. However, one may wonder what led Scadding to the choice of biological disadvantage as a morbidity-indicating criterion. It is possible that he set himself too ambitious a task in searching for a morbidity indicator that could be applied to the members of every species. Moreover, he may have wanted an indicator that seemed to be objectively ascertainable in some of its aspects. Biological disadvantage appeared to fit the bill. Some of its aspects, such as increased mortality or decreased vigour are certainly objectively ascertainable.

The concepts of illness, disease and morbus

Finally the question may be raised of whether biological disadvantage really is a characteristic of all diseases. It seems that there are exceptions to the rule. A case can certainly be made out for the thesis that there are diseases in which advantages outweigh any disadvantages in the long run. The most obvious examples are the immunities conferred by some mild infectious diseases. Indeed we make deliberate and generally successful use of those advantages, whenever we induce a mild disease in patients through vaccination or active immunization.

I adopted a different approach to the task of clarifying the concept of morbidity in general (Taylor, 1971, 1976). I did not aim at finding morbidity indicators that would be universally valid for all living organisms. I confined myself instead to the domain of human beings. This has had the advantage of providing access to the area of subjective experiences which cannot only be overtly displayed but are also verbally communicable.

Among possible morbidity indicators that immediately come to mind here are nociceptive experiences, ranging from discomfort and malaise to severe pain. They seem very adequate candidates, if we judge them by the etymology of some of the words used in designating ill people and their conditions. The Latin and Greek roots of such words as 'patient' or 'pathology', for instance, are terms referring to suffering, and so are such English words as 'dis-ease', 'ailment', or 'sickness'. Yet etymological considerations may merely unearth the fossils of past beliefs which have become obsolete in the modern world. Certainly there are feelings of suffering which occur in people of good health, such as the transient suffering occasioned by some athletic sports, by ascetic renunciations, and mild forms of punishment. Moreover, there are people who are commonly diagnosed as patients, though they do not complain of any nociceptive experiences or show any signs of them. Examples are unconscious patients, psychotics with ecstatic or grandiose delusions, or hypomanic patients with excessive feelings of well-being. The class of human patients thus overlaps with the class of persons having nociceptive experiences, but does not coincide with it. Nociceptive experiences therefore have certain shortcomings as morbidity indicators.

Another promising candidate for the clarification of human morbidity is the desire for therapeutic help. I have called this desire 'therapeutic concern' (Taylor, 1971, p. 359). At first sight, this concern seems to share most of the drawbacks of nociceptive experiences and has some additional ones of its own. There are, for example, psychotically depressed patients with the delusion that their sufferings are a deserved punishment and should not be treated, and there are paranoid psychotic patients with the delusion that their difficulties and troubles need no treatment, but will disappear with the removal of the evil influences responsible for them. However, these drawbacks of the concept of therapeutic concern are easily rectified. The therapeutic concern patients feel for themselves is not the only therapeutic concern which can indicate human morbidity. Patients can also arouse therapeutic concern for themselves in their social environment; that is, in the people around them. This can occur when the social environment learns from a patient about his symptoms or observes them independently, provided they are exteroceptible. In a patient who is unconscious or for other reasons unaware that he is in need of therapeutic help, the social environment's

69

therapeutic concern for him can be a primary morbidity indicator. Indeed with exteroceptible symptoms, the therapeutic concern of the social environment is a morbidity indicator for animals as well.

In the past, I included doctors among the social environment of patients. Morbidity was thus presented as being composed of the therapeutic concern patients felt for themselves and/or aroused for themselves in their social environment, and that these feelings were occasioned by certain statistically abnormal attributes. I have since realised that the concern for patients felt by doctors should be considered separately. Their feelings are not only a response to the accounts and complaints they obtain from patients and/or their social environment; they are modified by their knowledge of familiar clinical pictures and by their evaluations of diagnostic clinical signs for which they search in their clinical investigations. Moreover, their concern is not just a therapeutic one; it is also motivated by a desire to diagnose the form of morbidity involved and to assess the prognostic outlook. We shall therefore speak of the 'medical concern' of doctors and distinguish it from the therapeutic concern of lay persons.

The medical concern of doctors carries greater weight as a morbidity indicator than the therapeutic concern of lay persons. This is particularly so when the medical concern is based on clinical signs which are not accessible to lay observations and are known to be fairly reliable source indicators of a pathological background whose validity has been established through concordant research results.

We thus distinguish three morbidity indicators which transform certain statistically abnormal attributes into morbid ones. They are: a) a person's therapeutic concern for

Morbidity

himself, b) the therapeutic concern he arouses for himself in his social lay environment, and c) the medical concern for himself he elicits in his doctors.

Not every patient need have all three morbidity indicators. But every patient must have at least one of them. In logical language this means that the three morbidity indicators are disjunctively linked.

The empirical class of patients is an inexact class with blurred boundaries. There are borderline persons whose morbidity status cannot be readily decided, they cannot be assigned with any degree of confidence to either the empirical class of patients or the empirical class of non-patients. Their assignments vary in different cultures and have varied in different historical epochs. Among such borderline patients/non-patients, those with neurotic, psychotic, or psychopathic trends have had the most chequered fate and still continue to do so, depending on the communities they reside in. They can be denounced, disparaged and even punished as non-patients who are malingerers, hypochondriacs, ne'er-do-wells, or dissidents. They can also be accepted as patients who deserve sympathy and therapeutic help.

The fact that our morbidity indicators are psychological reactions in the form of therapeutic and/or medical concern makes them dependent on subjective and cultural vagaries. They certainly fall far short of ideal expectations and are thus open to criticism. Kendell (1975b, p. 11) has rejected them outright. For him, 'any definition of disease that boils down to "what people complain of" or "what doctors treat", or some combination of the two, is almost worse than no definition at all'. He based his rejection of our morbidity indicators on their dependence on 'changes in

71

The concepts of illness, disease and morbus

social attitudes and therapeutic optimism and . . . idiosyn-
cratic judgements by doctors or patients'. All this is, of
course, true. Yet when we look around the medical world,
our morbidity indicators seem to reflect what actually happens. Kendell himself is well aware of this, at least as far as
the diagnostic criteria of American and British psychiatrists
are concerned (e.g. Kendell *et al.*, 1971). Multi-national
investigations have highlighted the variability of diagnostic
criteria that exists especially in psychiatry (e.g. *The International Pilot Study of Schizophrenia* by the World Health Organization, Geneva, 1973). There is no reason to doubt that at
least some variability of diagnostic criteria exists also with
regard to non-psychiatric diseases.

Thus, until better morbidity indicators are found, our
criteria may have to serve despite their shortcomings. Yet
whatever criteria are adopted, they will all be defective in
one respect. They do not indicate 'true' morbidity, only
diagnosed or merely suspected morbidity; nor do they
characterize the members of the class of 'real' patients, only
those of the class of diagnosed or merely suspected
patients. Thus, when we speak in future of 'morbidity' and
'patients', these limitations will have to be kept in mind. It is
the price we have to pay for our lack of omniscience.

7

Morbi

When we add to the intension of a domain an attribute that is present in some domain members but not in others, that attribute becomes a classifying criterion. It divides the domain into a class whose members exhibit the classifying criterion and a class whose members do not. The two classes would be complementary, if there were no borderline candidates for them. Thus adding to the intension of the empirical domain of human beings the classifying criterion of morbidity, one of the resulting classes will be the class of all patients and the other the class of all non-patients (disregarding borderline candidates).

The class of all patients has morbidity as its intension. It is thus homogeneous in the sense that every patient is characterized by the attributes of morbidity to some extent and some degree. But this homogeneity is a purely taxonomic one; it does not indicate a homogeneity of causal derivation. It is a homogeneity that is a precondition of all class extensions.

Let us now take the empirical class of all patients as our domain. It has always been realized that its taxonomic homogeneity is of little practical value. It has therefore always been divided into many classes with the help of classifying criteria which consist of different configurations of morbid attributes. Each such configuration constitutes the intension of a particular class of patients. It is most commonly designated in English by the name 'disease'. The

73

concept thus named is, however, only a taxonomic entity which can be, and almost always is, polygenic in its causal derivation. Only a few diseases are monogenic entities whose pathological onset has already been established.

Through the formidable influence of Virchow and under the impressive impact of the discoveries of pathological anatomists, the term 'disease' began to assume a new and narrowed technical sense; it began to be limited to the designation of particular configurations of pathological abnormalities. In other words, diseases were identified with Virchowian disease entities. Yet these were still only taxonomic disease entities, though they gained increasing importance as classifying criteria in the empirical domain of patients. Completely new classes of patients therefore made their appearance. They had 'organic' diseases which had names descriptive of their pathological origin rather than their clinical appearance. Classes of patients whose classifying criteria had been clinical manifestations (e.g. dropsy, biliousness, jaundice, ileus, or consumption) began to fall apart and were replaced by classes of patients whose classifying criteria were Virchowian disease entities (e.g. cardiac dilatation, nephritis, hepatitis, gastric ulcer, appendicitis, or pulmonary tuberculosis). Conceptual and terminological innovations swept all across the nosological board and altered it out of all recognition.

Once the term 'disease' was firmly established in its narrowed sense, it parted company with terms that had previously been more or less synonymous with it. It became reserved for pathological configurations of abnormalities in the cells, organs, and tissues of patients. Clinical manifestations were something quite separate; they were symptoms and signs from which clinicians could diagnostically infer

Morbi

pathological diseases. The confirmation or rejection of such
diagnostic inferences, however, remained for a long time in
the hands of pathologists who, in the post mortem room,
became the ultimate arbiter of the diagnostic acumen of
clinicians. In due course, clinicians succeeded in regaining
much of their diagnostic authority through keeping their
patients alive for longer and through finding pathological
source indicators to add to the clinical signs already available to them. However, they now needed a name which
was specifically applicable to clinical manifestations and not
to pathological abnormalities which had already usurped
the name 'disease'. The names 'symptomatology' and
'semeiology' were advocated at one time for this purpose.
However, they failed to find general favour. They were in
any case too long and cumbersome. The helpful suggestion
has recently been made by Feinstein (1967, pp. 24f) to use
the term 'illness' in the special technical sense of indicating
only clinical manifestations. Indeed such usage is in accordance with a trend that can already be discerned in much
medical writing.

Feinstein's approach to our problem deserves to be considered in detail. He remarks: 'A clinician observes at least
three different types of data. The first type of data describes
a *disease* in morphologic, chemical, microbiologic,
physiologic, or other impersonal terms. The second type of
data describes a *host* in whom the disease occurs. The
description of the host's environmental background
includes both the personal properties of the host before the
disease began (such as age, race, sex, and education) and
also the properties of the host's external surroundings (such
as geographic location, occupation, and financial and social
status). The third type of data describes the *illness* that

The concepts of illness, disease and morbus

occurs in the interaction between the disease and its environmental host. The illness consists of clinical phenomena; the host's subjective sensations, which are called "symptoms", and certain findings, called "signs", which are discerned objectively during the physical examination of the diseased host.' (Italics in the original.)

Feinstein's distinction between disease and host is obviously a reflection of Virchow's view that 'disease is a living entity that leads a parasitic existence . . . [in] the otherwise healthy body'. This otherwise healthy body was Virchow's host concept. Feinstein's is wider, since it refers not only to the body of the patient, but also to his personality, social setting, and environmental circumstances. Yet his interpretation of illness as 'occurring in the interaction between the disease and its environmental host' is not entirely satisfactory. It seems to imply that the pathological data composing disease are not interactions. Such an implication is unjustified. Pathological data are also the products of interactions which start with the first reaction of the host organism to the event that constitutes the pathological onset. They continue in a complex series of interactions between the host organism and the various pathological effects produced by previous interactions. It is only in the end that the interactions also give rise to those manifestations which form a clinical illness.

In thus distinguishing between a clinical illness and a pathological disease, we have split into two parts the morbid attributes whose configuration forms the intension of a particular empirical class of patients. We thus can no longer say that the intension of a particular class of patients is a disease. It may be a disease or an illness or both according to the stage pathological processes have reached or according

76

to our ignorance of the disease behind a manifest clinical illness. As a result we need a special name to denote both the illness and disease components or just one of them, dependent on what we know of the intension of a particular class of patients. The expression 'particular form of morbidity' which we used before could serve the purpose. However, a shorter expression is preferable. It is therefore proposed to use the term *morbus* instead. It is a term that has the advantage of not being any more in modern medical parlance and yet being sufficiently familiar to convey the meaning which fits our requirements. The intension of a particular class of patients is thus a particular morbus. Such a morbus is an abstract taxonomic entity.

Morbi are polythetic intensions. Therefore, the individual members of an empirical class of patients need only exhibit a large proportion, or at least a significant portion, of its morbus. In the clinic, we deal with empirical classes whose concrete entities are patients; in the operating theatres and the laboratories, we may deal with empirical classes whose concrete entities are only parts of patients. Yet in these situations we do not deal with morbi, since morbi are abstract entities. For the same reason, we can only treat patients or, at the very least, those concrete manifestations of their morbi which are still present in them. We cannot treat past manifestations of a morbus which have long since been superseded. The frequently made demands that we should treat causes rather than clinical symptoms make sense only when those causes are understood to be pathological events which are concomitant with clinical symptoms. Causes which are past and vanished events in the life of a morbus are no longer accessible to any therapeutic efforts.

The concepts of illness, disease and morbus

Though we cannot treat in the clinic abstract morbi nor any of the abstract morbid attributes composing them, we can treat *of* them when we turn from the empirical domain of patients to the theoretical domains which are considered in medical papers and text-books.

There are two kinds of theoretical domains. There is, first of all, the domain of morbid attributes. It can be subdivided in various ways merely for the practical purpose of bringing order into the discussion of morbid attributes. Such discussion is mainly concerned with three points: a) the manner in which morbid attributes present themselves or have to be elicited, b) their occurrence in different morbi, and c) their role in the differential diagnosis of morbi.

The other theoretical domain is that of morbi. It is usually known as 'the nosological domain'. The particular morbi in it are, for the most part, only taxonomic entities with origins that are polygenic. The subdivision of the nosological domain again serves merely practical purposes, such as distinguishing between theoretical classes of medical, surgical, gynaecological, dermatological, psychiatric, and other morbi. We cannot, however, establish among any of the theoretical classes in the nosological domain a hierarchical order such as had been possible in the theoretical domain of biological taxa. There is no evolutionary background in the nosological domain which makes hierarchical arrangements feasible. Yet several attempts were made in the past to construct hierarchical nosological systems. Such attempts had their heyday in the eighteenth century and were quite obviously inspired by Linnaeus' *Systema Naturae* which first appeared in 1735 and was cumulatively enlarged in twelve subsequent editions. Chief among the classifiers of morbi was Boissier de Sauvages who was, like Linnaeus, a botanist and physician. The final edition of his classifications was published in 1763 under the title *Nosologia Methodica Sistens Morborum Classes, Genera et Species* ('Methodical Nosology Consisting of the Classes, Genera, and Species of Morbi'). He mentioned 2400 individual morbi, hundreds of Genera, 40 Orders, and 10 Classes. Boissier de Sauvages had many followers. Linnaeus himself was among them.

Eventually the futility of forcing individual morbi into a hierarchical scheme was realized. The classification of morbi began to be put on a more pragmatic basis which aimed at clinical, heuristic, and administrative merits. The first to lay down general principles for such a pragmatic classification was William Farr whose *Report on the Nomenclature and Statistical Classification of Diseases for Statistical Returns* appeared in 1856. The modern off-shoot of Farr's work is the *International Classification of Diseases* (ICD) which is revised every ten years under the auspices of the World Health Organization.

If we were omniscient, then every individual morbus in the nosological domain would be monogenic. It would have a specific pathological onset and specific radical source indicators revealing that onset. It would be differentiated from other morbi by these two constituents among its many morbid attributes. As we are not omniscient, most of the individual morbi in the nosological domain, and therefore considered in our text-books, are still polygenic in origin. They are entities only in a taxonomic sense. Their configurations have gaps which reflect the limits of medical knowledge at particular times. Such polygenic morbi owe their membership in the nosological domain to fortuitous circumstances.

The concepts of illness, disease and morbus

For the most part, doctors live contentedly with the incompleteness of their diagnostic knowledge. Yet sometimes such incompleteness becomes sufficiently embarrassing to be acknowledged in the name of a morbus whose pathological derivations remain hidden. The name then contains an epithet that admits, or at least hints at, lacunae in diagnostic knowledge. The frankest epithet that has been used is 'cryptogenic'. Yet such frankness is neither widespread nor popular. It dims the halo of superior knowledge and therapeutic promise with which suffering humanity tends to endow medical men. There are other epithets which are not quite as frank and outspoken. That is why some polygenic morbi have been called 'idiopathic', i.e. pathological in themselves irrespective of pathogenesis (e.g. 'idiopathic' epilepsy or ulcerative colitis). Other epithets hark back to the belief in spontaneous generation which Pasteur had experimentally dispelled in 1860. We therefore have some 'spontaneous' morbi (e.g. 'spontaneous' Cushing's syndrome or pneumothorax). Similar adjectives are 'essential' (e.g. 'essential' hypertension), 'primary' (e.g. 'primary' goitre), or 'autonomous' (e.g. 'autonomous' aldosteronism). Whether a morbus is frankly called 'cryptogenic' or not, we sometimes acknowledge the fact that the cryptogenesis of a morbus can be a matter of degree. That is why we sometimes speak of 'symptomatic' morbi to indicate that a morbus of which we know usually only the clinical component can occasionally be the outcome of a known pathological lesion, of a disease.

Most morbi begin their nosological career as taxonomic entities whose pathogenesis is so obscure that they have no known disease components. They consist only of clinical illnesses, composed of symptoms which are not pathologi-

80

cal source indicators. The clinical symptoms in question attracted the attention of lay people and physicians in the first place, because they were conspicuous, roused therapeutic and medical concern, and, though abnormal by population standards, occurred in a sufficient number of people to encourage the belief that they indicated a special class of patients. Examples were fevers, rashes, epilepsy, apoplexy, asthma, dropsy, and the like.

Let us take fever as an example of one such conspicuous symptom. It is still regarded as clinically so helpful that temperature charts continue to adorn many of our hospital beds, even when they are occupied by non-febrile patients. Yet febrile illness is the clinical component of many morbi, most of them only partly known and polygenic. It is a clinical necessity that the empirical class of febrile patients is divided into sub-classes of increasing diagnostic and therapeutic usefulness. For this purpose, adequate classifying criteria have to be found. The search for them may begin with a study of the course various fever curves can take. They can be acute or chronic, continuous for several days, remitting, intermitting, relapsing, and so on. Yet, for the most part, fever curves indicate polygenic morbi. It is only occasionally that a particular fever curve is eventually found to be diagnostically highly significant for a monogenic morbus as happened, for instance, with the recurrent rigors of quartan malaria.

Another method of finding classifying criteria for the subdivision of the class of febrile patients relies on the clinical observation of any symptoms accompanying fever in the hope of establishing particular configurations. Again there have been some chance successes even in antiquity. Mumps, for example, was described by Hippocrates and smallpox by Galen. However, clinical observation by itself without the help of pathogenic research has had few achievements to its credit in the many centuries during which it was practised. Today, when the pathogenic research of a particular morbus is still drawing a blank, sophisticated statistical methods are enlisted to refine clinical observation. But such methods cannot by themselves transform clinical manifestations into pathological, or even radical, source indicators. This needs assistance from pathogenic research.

As long as conspicuous clinical symptoms were almost the sole components of morbi, the name of a morbus was often descriptive of its characteristic symptom. For example, the morbus whose characteristic symptom was an acute fever used to be called 'acuta febris' by mediaeval physicians. This was shortened to 'acuta', a term which entered the English language as 'ague' in the seventeenth century. The morbus whose characteristic symptoms were attacks of one-sided headaches was originally called 'hemicrania' and this became 'megrim' and later 'migraine' in English. Morbi of this kind are certainly polygenic for the most part. Yet occasionally they turn out eventually to be monogenic as happened, for instance, in the case of the morbus called 'whooping cough'.

The naming of morbi is unavoidable for the purposes of identification and communication. But names have their pitfalls and difficulties. The greatest trouble with many of the names used for morbi is their ambiguity. If a morbus name is derived from its characteristic clinical symptom, ambiguity is inevitable. 'Whooping cough', for example, designates the clinical symptom of a cough followed by a whooping inspiration; it also designates the clinical illness associated with this symptom; and finally it designates the whole morbus which has not only an illness component but a disease component as well. Obviously such ambiguities are not conducive to clear thinking; they may give rise to confusion and apparent contradictions.

Let us see how the naming of a newly discovered morbus has fared. The first inkling of its existence came in 1934, when the Norwegian biochemist and physician, A. Fölling, was asked to examine two mentally subnormal siblings whose urine had a peculiar odour. He found that their urine contained an abnormal substance, namely phenylpyruvic acid. He found the same abnormality in a number of other mentally subnormal persons. There thus existed in the empirical class of mentally subnormal patients a sub-class characterized by the urinary excretion of phenylpyruvic acid. Fölling christened the intension of this sub-class 'imbecillitas phenylpyrouvica' and others spoke of 'phenylpyruvic oligophrenia'. Both these terms were descriptive of the clinical illness with its two main constituents: the symptom of mental subnormality and the sign of the urinary excretion of phenylpyruvic acid. There was no ambiguity here, because the terms mentioned only the symptoms of a clinical illness and nothing else was known of the morbus. However, the hypothesis was formed that the clinical illness had a metabolic abnormality as its pathological cause. This hypothesis by itself did not convert the clinical sign of the urinary excretion of phenylpyruvic acid into a pathological source indicator, since it still lacked the validity and reliability required of source indicators. But some of these requirements were soon supplied. The clinical sign was found to be a valid and reliable source indicator of too high a level of phenylalanine in the blood. Moreover, there were indications that this high level was due to a deficiency in metabolizing this particular amino acid, because the urine of these patients contained not only phenylpyruvic acid, but also other phenylketones which are metabolites of phenylalanine. The metabolic abnormality was due to the homozygous inheritance of a pathological recessive gene. The morbus in question was thus monogenic, the pathological onset being the formation of a zygote through the fusion of two gametes which each contained the pathological gene. Penrose & Quastel (1937) suggested the name 'phenylketonuria' for the morbus to bring the nomenclature into line with that of other inborn errors of metabolism, such as alkaptonuria, cystinuria, or pentosuria. This name has found general acceptance, especially in its acronymic form 'PKU'. But since the name was derived from the clinical sign of excreting phenylketones in the urine it had the flaw of ambiguity, signifying the clinical sign, the clinical illness, and also the morbus as a whole.

From such ambiguity, there is only a small step to apparent self-contradiction. The parents of PKU patients, being heterozygous for the pathological gene, can have PKU (the clinical sign) after a meal rich in phenylalanine, though they do not have PKU (the illness or the morbus). Similarly, a PKU patient, when on a diet poor in phenylalanine from his earliest days, still has PKU (the morbus) without PKU (the illness or the clinical sign).

Confusion can get even worse confounded when medical men are not on their guard. In 1873, Sir W. W. Gull noticed a particular clinical illness to which he gave the unflattering title 'cretinoid condition of middle-aged women' (Singer & Underwood, 1962, p. 524). Soon afterwards, W. M. Ord observed (Singer & Underwood, 1962, p. 524) that patients with this illness had a non-pitting oedema due to the sub-cutaneous accumulation of some mucinous substance. He called this clinical sign 'myxoedema' and, without fail, the name was ambiguously applied to the associated illness as well. In due course, the sign of myxoedema and other cognate signs turned out to be source indicators of a pathological condition which consisted of various structural lesions of the thyroid gland and caused it to function defi-ciently. This pathological condition constituted a disease which was called 'hypothyroidism'. There was thus a partially known morbus with an illness and a disease com-ponent. But the morbus had no name of its own. So it borrowed the two available names of 'myxoedema' and 'hypothyroidism'. The end result was that the two names became synonymous as far as the morbus was concerned. In other respects, they remained heteronymous. The door was thus opened for the appearance of paradoxical state-ments, such as: 'Hypothyroidism sometimes occurs as part of the presentation of Graves' syndrome, with coincident exophthalmus and pretibial myxoedema' (Cecil-Loeb, 1971, p. 1768). Since Graves' syndrome is the clinical illness of the disease of hyperthyroidism, the statement seems to assert that hy*po*thyroidism can be part of hy*per*thyroidism. Yet 'hypothyroidism' here merely denotes the occasional clini-cal sign of pretibial myxoedema in patients with Graves' syndrome.

It is impossible to rid medical terms of their ambiguities. After all, many terms in natural languages acquire a diver-sity of meanings of which dictionaries keep a systematic record. Yet even if we could ensure that any terms we use are univocal, we would still have to contend with other vagaries of name relations. Philosophers and logicians have

The concepts of illness, disease and morbus

wrangled with these problems for centuries. In the Middle Ages, for instance, there were scholastic philosophers, known as 'nominalists', who maintained that concrete entities had real existence but abstract entities did not. Since univocal name relations must be between an expression and a particular entity, the only 'proper' names were those that designated a concrete entity. General and abstract names designated nothing; they were, as Roscellin is supposed to have said in the eleventh century, mere *flatus vocis*, mere vocal noises. Scholastic philosophers of a different persuasion were known as 'realists'. They maintained that abstract entities were special substances which existed as pure forms and essences in a supersensible realm. The Catholic Church lent its dogmatic authority to the tenets of scholastic realism, since some theological doctrines (e.g. that of the Holy Trinity) were based on them. These tenets thus had a long life in popular thought, even after they had been abandoned among most philosophers. That is the reason why Sydenham, in the seventeenth century, still regarded such class entities as biological species and specific diseases as each having 'a substantial form, or essence' which was imperfectly embodied or instantiated in the members of a biological species or the patients with a specific disease.

The tenets of scholastic realism were eclipsed among philosophers through the teaching of William of Occam (of Occam's razor fame) in the fourteenth century. He evolved a modified form of nominalism, known as 'conceptualism'. According to it, nothing existed in physical reality apart from concrete entities, but there were similarities between concrete entities which could be recognized by preformed concepts in the human mind, concepts which functioned as 'natural signs' or *intentiones animae* of these similarities.

General and abstract names could be used to designate those concepts.

Today, a concept is not regarded as something that exists preformed in the human mind and mirrors similarities between concrete entities. In logical contexts, it is usually understood as an abstract entity which is formed by the human mind, but must be differentiated from any psychological experience of it as a cognitive phenomenon in an individual mind at a particular time. Carnap (1956, p. 21), for instance, states: 'The term "concept" will be used here as a common designation for properties, relations, and similar entities. . . . For this term it is especially important to stress the fact that it is not to be understood in a mental sense, that is, as referring to a process of imagining, thinking, conceiving, or the like, but rather to something objective that is found in nature and that is expressed in language by a designator of nonsentential form [i.e. by general names, class names, attribute names, and the like]'. One can quarrel with the use of the term 'nature' in Carnap's statement. It seems more satisfactory to regard the kind of concepts with which logicians deal as abstract entities that exist in inter-subjective cultural realities. Such a view would take account of the fact that different cultures can evolve different concepts, that the same concepts are designated by different names in different cultures, and that the same name may refer to different concepts through changes in cultural outlooks.

In the history of medicine, some nosological concepts have certainly come and gone with cultural changes of medical doctrines and theories. When a nosological concept vanishes or changes, its name may yet remain on the scene. Indeed some nosological names have enjoyed

The concepts of illness, disease and morbus

extraordinary longevity despite frequent changes in the concepts they designate. 'Influenza' is an example of this. It signified originally the concept of some noxious 'influence' exerted by certain planetary constellations which were thought to cause seasonal epidemics of certain symptoms. Today this original meaning of 'influenza' is so obsolete that it is no more than a historical curiosity. The same can be said of 'hysteria' which once meant a pathologically wandering womb, and of 'rheumatism' which referred to the mucous rheum that emerged from the nose in a head cold and was supposed to seep into joints and muscles, making them swollen and painful when the cold noxa affected the body instead of the head. Of course, there have also been nosological concepts whose demise left their names without any medical connotation or usefulness. This has happened, for instance, to such diagnoses as 'spleen', 'gastroptosis', 'fibrositis', 'vapours', 'shellshock', 'phrenitis', 'melancholia', and so on.

The name of a taxonomic morbus is essentially the name of the intension of a particular class of patients. We do not have special abstract names for these classes. Also, there are only a few general names for the members of certain patient classes, such as 'leper', 'albino', 'epileptic', or 'schizophrenic'. When such a general name is available, we could construct an abstract class name from it, for example 'leperkind' in analogy to 'mankind'. We would then say 'a leper belongs to leperkind' instead of 'a leper has leprosy'. This may be of some linguistic interest; it certainly would not enrich medical discussions.

It has become a linguistic convention that biological species are designated by abstract class names, whereas morbi are designated by abstract intension names. A class of biological species is thus a class of classes, but a class of morbi is a class of intensions. Does this difference matter?

This kind of question has, of course, been discussed among philosophers and logicians. Alfred N. Whitehead and Bertrand Russell in their *Principia Mathematica* (1927, p. 72) remarked: 'It is an old dispute whether formal logic should concern itself mainly with intensions or with extensions. In general, logicians whose training was mainly philosophical have decided for intensions, while those whose training was mainly mathematical have decided for extensions. The fact seems to be that, while mathematical logic requires extensions, philosophical logic refuses to supply anything except intensions. Our theory of classes recognizes and reconciles these two apparently opposite facts by showing that an extension (which is the same as a class) is an incomplete symbol, whose use always acquires its meaning through a reference to intension'.

The last sentence in this quotation illustrates that even Homer sometimes nods. It is carelessly phrased. An extension is never a symbol of any kind, it is only designated by a symbol. In the notation of *Principia Mathematica* classes are described in a way that may be translated into English as 'the class of all those domain members that are characterized by a particular intension'. If the domain members are patients, then the class of lepers would be indicated by the expression 'the class of all those patients that are characterized by leprosy' (which happens to be a monogenic morbus).

In their *Introduction* to the second edition of *Principia Mathematica*, Whitehead & Russell go even further (p. xxxix) by suggesting that there is no reason for distinguishing between notations for intensions and extensions, because both notations have the same meaning. All that was really needed was a notation for intensions. They retained the class notations, merely because it was sometimes more convenient. They thus gave an incidental stamp of approval to the medical custom of using morbus names instead of class names. At the same time, there would be no significance in the use of class names for biological taxa other than the convenience of conforming with a long-established convention.

Not all logicians readily agree with the conceptualist view adopted by Whitehead and Russell. Some are reluctant to accept any abstract entities, such as class concepts, class intensions, propositions, conclusions, beliefs, and the like. Such logicians dream of achieving one day a system of logic, especially of mathematical logic, which will be entirely in accordance with the doctrines of scholastic nominalism. One of these logicians is W. V. Quine. In his *Mathematical Logic* (1961, p. 121), we read: 'Discourse in general, mathematical and otherwise, involves continual reference to abstract entities of this sort – classes or properties. One may prefer to regard abstractions as fictions or manners of speaking; one may hope to find a method whereby all ostensible reference to abstract entities can be explained as mere shorthand for a more basic idiom involving reference only to concrete objects (in some sense or other). Such a nominalistic program presents extreme difficulty, . . . however, it is not known to be impossible. . . . Meanwhile, however, we have no choice but to admit those abstract entities as part of our ultimate subject matter'.

Taxonomic morbi are quite obviously the kind of abstract entities that would be acceptable to even those logicians who have nominalistic leanings. From a conceptualistic point of view, we can certainly credit morbi with existence in the cultural reality of medical thought. Yet medical men do mislead themselves occasionally by misjudged nominal-istic arguments. We find, for example, this argument in Scadding (1967): 'Since the exact description of a disease depends on the defining characteristics we choose to adopt for it, it seems to me impossible to think of diseases as having any sort of independent existence; . . . and I think we must adopt an uncompromisingly nominalist view-point'. This passage prompted F. S. A. Doran to write a letter to *The Lancet* (1967) in which he said: 'To analyze something that does not exist is, surely, a pointless waste of time'.

This detour into metaphysical disputes of past ages was completely mistaken. To realize this, we merely have to replace the term 'disease' in Scadding's statement by a term that refers to a patient with a particular disease. Let us choose a disease whose defining characteristics have recently been the subject of an international study conducted by the World Health Organization (1973) in which nine countries and a large number of highly expert investigators took part. It was a study concerning the disease of schizophrenia. The re-phrased statement by Scadding then reads: 'Since the exact description of a schizophrenic patient depends on the defining characteristics we choose to adopt for him, it seems to me impossible to think of a schizophrenic patient as having any sort of independent existence'.

This was obviously not the point that Scadding wished to make. His aim rather seems to have been to point out how arbitrary the composition of a polygenic and only partially known morbus is, since its configuration is established by defining characteristics which happen to be available and perhaps internationally accepted.

8

Molecular morbi

Among cryptogenic morbi, there are some which are so inadequately known that we remain entirely ignorant of the pathological origin of their illness components. In some of these morbi, no disease components are known at all. Yet a cryptogenic morbus must have a disease component; there must be a pathological basis for its symptoms and signs. If that basis has not been detected, testable hypotheses and untestable speculations come into their own. In the past, for instance, clinicians often hypothesized that the pathological basis could consist of transient inflammations. That was a time when diagnosis of myocarditis, fibrositis, and meningitis (or, more cautiously, meningismus) were popular among clinicians, if they could find no adequate reasons for clinical complaints. But when pathologists tested the hypothesis, they proved it unfounded. In most patients with such diagnoses, when they could be examined pathologically, there was no evidence that inflammations were, or had been, present. In due course, therefore, the frequency of such diagnoses went down. Clinicians became more circumspect and learned to rely on source-indicating signs, before diagnosing inflammations.

Other hypotheses about illnesses which had no detectable pathological basis at necropsy were more firmly based on evidence. When there were no structural lesions to account for clinical manifestations, there was still the possibility that morbid abnormalities of certain biological functions were responsible for them. Since all biological functions cease at death, they cannot be observed at post mortem investigations. Pathological anatomists could at best infer morbid functional abnormalities, if there had been structural consequences of them. It is only in the living patient that morbid functional abnormalities can be firmly established, provided there are source indicators of them among available clinical signs.

This trend of thought gave rise to the discipline of pathophysiology which complemented the findings of pathological anatomy. Yet pathophysiological events seemed fundamentally different from the structural lesions which were disease entities in a Virchowian sense. This fundamental difference was reflected in a linguistic convention that denied the term 'disease' to pathophysiological events. They were called *functional disorders*. In the nosological domain, the class of functional disorders was strictly distinguished from the class of organic diseases in the second half of the nineteenth century. The class of functional disorders was divided into several sub-classes according to the biological organs or systems involved and whether functional activities were increased, reduced, or went astray. There were therefore disorders of cardiac functions (e.g. paroxysmal tachycardia), of vascular functions (e.g. hyper- or hypotension), of gastric functions (e.g. hyper- or hypoacidity, hyper- or hypotonus), of metabolic functions (e.g. of carbohydrate metabolism), of endocrine functions (e.g. hyper- or hypothyroidism), of immune functions (e.g. allergy), of nerve functions (e.g. neuralgia), of psychological functions (e.g. intellectual deficiency, neurosis), and of many other functions.

The diagnosis of a functional disorder did not, of course,

exclude the possible occurrence of causally related organic lesions. In the first place, a usually functional disorder could be occasionally 'symptomatic' of an organic disease. For example the functional disorder of carbohydrate metabolism could in a few patients be 'symptomatic' of chronic pancreatitis. In the second place, all functional disorders could have organic lesions as consequences. Even functional psychological disorders could have such consequences through suicidal attempts, self-mutilations, or accident proneness.

Today the strict distinction between functional disorders and organic diseases is on its way out in most nosological areas. Indeed one gets the impression that the words 'disorder' and 'disease' are often used interchangeably, where 'disorder' had been obligatory before. For example, Bomford & Mason, writing in Price's *Textbook of the Practice of Medicine* (1973, p. 496), inform us: 'Diabetes mellitus is *not a disease*, but includes a variety of related *disorders* of medicine . . .' (my italics). In a similar vein, P. K. Bondy writes in Cecil-Loeb's *Textbook of Medicine* (1971, p. 1639): 'Diabetes mellitus is a generalized chronic metabolic *disorder*. . . . If the course of the *disease* is indolent . . .' (my italics).

It is only in neurology and psychiatry that the distinction between the two terms is still very much alive. We find, for instance, Cottom defining trigeminal neuralgia in Price's *Textbook* (1973, p. 1171) as 'a *disorder* confined to paroxysms of intense pain in the distribution of the trigeminal nerve only, without sensory loss or other evidence of *organic disease* of the nerve' (my italics). Shepherd, who contributes the section on psychological medicine to Price's *Textbook* (1973, pp. 1331ff), has a subheading entitled 'Psychiatric Disorders Associated with Organic Diseases' (p. 1341). The comparable section in Cecil-Loeb's *Textbook* (1971, pp. 83ff) is headed 'Disorders of the Nervous System and Behavior', though one of the contributors to the section, McHugh (p. 107), makes a special attempt to define 'the concept of disease in psychiatry'.

The belief that there is a fundamental difference between functional disorders and organic diseases is thus still lingering on. This is probably due to the fact that there is a long history of myths, legends, and speculations behind the belief and they hark back to early cultures of mankind. It is in essence the history of the concepts of energy and force. The concepts still have an aura of mystery about them even for the atomic scientists of today who often sidestep the issues involved by talking of the 'interactions' they can observe rather than of the explanatory force-particles behind them.

The aura of mystery is even deeper in biology, because there are still echoes alive today of ancient, and sometimes not so ancient, beliefs that the life force is different from all other forces in the world. The life force was originally linked with the air we breathe, because life stops when we stop breathing. We read in Genesis 2:7: 'And the Lord God formed man of the dust of the ground, and breathed into his nostrils the breath of life; and man became a living soul'. Breath, life, soul, and mind were thus coupled together. We find the same coupling in Greek and Roman cultures, for the words used for mind, soul, and the principle of life are etymologically linked with those used for breath and air. 'Psyche' was originally the Greek word for breath; 'spirit' is derived from the Latin 'spirare'; 'exspirare' (or 'expire' in its Anglicized form) means not only to breathe out, but also to die; and 'anima' was the original Latin word for wind and

The concepts of illness, disease and morbus

air. 'Animistic', or 'vitalistic', doctrines of a life force were energetically propagated by some leading physicians of the eighteenth century. They are by no means without influence today, not only among the general public that believes in a life of the soul after the death of the body, but also among doctors who follow certain 'psychodynamic' theories which separate psychic from physical forces and presume that conflicting psychic energies can be unconsciously converted into physical symptoms in so-called 'conversion' hysteria.

An offshoot of these doctrines was the firmly held belief that there was an unbridgeable gap between inorganic substances of mineral origin and organic substances of biological origin. The latter were thought to be unproducible except with the help of the life force. This firmly held conviction was shattered in 1828, when Friedrich Wöhler, very much to his own surprise, obtained the organic substance urea by the simple process of heating the inorganic substance ammonium cyanate.

According to the gospel of Galenic teaching which reigned supreme in Western medicine for nearly 1500 years, the life force manifested itself in three kinds of subtle spirits. There were the 'natural' spirits which, together with blood, were continually created in the liver. There were the 'vital' spirits which originated in the left ventricle and were transported with the blood to peripheral organs, where blood was burned up producing poisonous fumes that were exhaled by the lungs. Finally, there were the 'animal' spirits (i.e. anima-derived spirits) which were produced in the cavities of the brain and flowed through the nerves to organs, where they could initiate movement and sensation.

When Galenic teaching was finally superseded, only

animal spirits lingered on under various guises in medical thought. Indeed they gained the semblance of scientific respectability from an unexpected quarter in the eighteenth century. In his *General Scholium* of 1713, Sir Isaac Newton suggested that there is 'an electric and elastic spirit' that permeates all physical bodies. He went on to say that 'all sensation is excited, and the members of animal bodies move . . . by vibrations of this spirit, mutually propagated along the solid filaments of the nerves, from the outward organs of the sense to the brain, and from the brain into the muscles'. (Quoted from Wightman, 1958, p. 138.)

Newton's speculative remarks were noted and elaborated by influential physicians. There was, for instance, Friedrich Hoffmann, the German physician after whom Rubella is still called 'German' measles. He attributed to Newton's 'electric and elastic spirit', which was then known as 'nervous ether', the capacity of maintaining the tonus of bodily functions. When Hoffmann diagnosed that a person did not have enough nervous ether in his organism, he prescribed 'tonics', such as a mixture of about two parts of alcohol and one part of ether (not the 'nervous' variety but the chemical substance di-ethylether) which is still available as 'Hoffmann's drops' in Germany. Tonics of one kind or another have remained in favour with the medical and lay public, though they have nowadays lost much ground to the suggestively named 'vitamins' which seem to hark back to the 'vital' spirits of yore.

Hoffmann's theories influenced William Cullen who held chairs of medicine in Glasgow and Edinburgh in the eighteenth century. He was the author of a famous text-book entitled *Nosology, or a Systematic Arrangement of Diseases by Classes, Orders, Genera, and Species with the Distinguishing*

The concepts of illness, disease and morbus

Characteristics of Each (1772), showing that he was one of the hierarchical classifiers. He taught that the health of the body depended in part on 'nervous' power, force, or energy. He also coined the word 'neuroses' for a class of diseases depending on a 'general affection of the nervous system and of those powers of the system upon which sense and motion more especially depend' (Cullen, 1777).

Cullen's pupil, John Brown, went further and maintained that diseases could be divided into 'sthenic' and 'asthenic' ones, the former being due to an excess of nervous energy, the latter to a deficiency of it. This 'Brunonian' theory had a long and remarkable life. Its heyday was in the second half of the nineteenth century. The asthenic morbus *par excellence* entered the nosological world in 1869, when it was described by the New York psychiatrist, G. M. Beard, and named 'neurasthenia'. He spoke of people with too much nervous energy ('millionaires of nerve force') and their poor counterparts, the neurasthenics, with too little of it (Beard, 1880). Before long, the diagnosis of neurasthenia reached epidemic proportions, especially in America. Since then, it has faded away and today it is only an occasional diagnostic label *faute de mieux*.

Although the concept of nervous energy has thus been bandied about by many generations of doctors, its mysterious and other-worldly aura has apparently never quite vanished. True, it began to be endowed with more mundane attributes in the eighteenth century, at first through the conjectures of Newton and, towards the end of it, through the speculations of Galvani that there are two forms of electric energy: the usual physical kind and a special animal variety. Galvani thought that animal electricity was secreted by the brain, conveyed through the nerves to muscles

98

Molecular morbi

and there stored as in a Leyden jar, until it was released and caused muscular contractions. It was soon proved by Volta that Galvani was mistaken. There was only one kind of electricity and that was the familiar physical kind. In 1843, the German physiologist, du Bois-Reymond, showed that this physical kind of electricity occurred in the form of 'action currents', whenever nerves and muscles were active. It seemed then that it was electric power that constituted the nerve force. Electrotherapy which had already been a favourite with many doctors for many years began to flourish as never before in the hope that the body could thus be supplied with nervous strength.

It was at about the same time that biochemistry began to emerge as a special branch of chemistry. Metabolic functions were gradually clarified and it began to be realized that the body was supplied with chemical energy through oxidative processes which were at first pictured as forms of slow combustion. Today, we know that oxidative processes are based on the release of electrons from molecules. It is also known today that there is no fundamental difference between chemical and electric energy, since they both have their origin in the electromagnetic forces which bind electrons to atomic nuclei. However, to the physicians of the nineteenth century, it seemed that the body had at its disposal two different kinds of energy of which one was generated by slow combustion and the other by special processes in the nervous system. The ideas entertained were, however, vague, varied, and conflicting. There was a common belief that the central nervous system contained special centres which regulated the functions of the body's organs by the distribution of nervous energy. The highest centres were those of conscious voluntary experiences in which will

99

power and judgment resided. They could (or was it 'should'?) keep in check the conscious involuntary centres through which pleasant or painful sensations and instinctual or emotional urges were experienced. They could exert some minor control over the automatically functioning respiratory centres, but none at all over the unconscious centres regulating bodily functions autonomically.

One may venture to assume that in the mechanistic age of the industrial revolution the body was viewed by analogy with a factory floor in which the various machines (organs) had their own power supply (through blood circulation and chemical combustion). The activities of the various machines were initiated and co-ordinated according to an automatic schedule (in unconscious nervous centres) or in response to instructions from the board room (conscious nervous centres). Things could go wrong on the factory floor in three ways: a) through a structural (organic) breakdown in machines or their power supplies, b) through errors creeping into an automatic schedule which threw co-ordination out of gear (functional autonomic disorders), and c) through unrealistic or muddled instructions from the board room (nervous and mental disorders).

But the nineteenth century was also the Virchowian age of pathological anatomy. Therefore, if there were centres in the central nervous system, they had to have their special locations and structures. Speculation was rife, especially about the centres of consciousness. Leading physiologists were convinced that those centres had their locations in the medulla. Later, they placed them in the sensory ganglia and particularly the 'optic' thalamus. It was only in the 1870s, through the influence of such workers as Fritsch and Hitzig, Hughlings Jackson, and Ferrier, that conscious centres were assigned to the cerebral cortex. The search was on for structural lesions in the cortex and the rest of the brain which would account for those illnesses of motor, sensory, and psychological functions that had stubbornly remained cryptogenic. The result was the emergence of neuropathology and neurology. Hitherto unknown neuropathological lesions were detected together with their neurological signs and illnesses. There were even mental patients in whom neuropathological diseases were present. Foremost among them were patients with general paralysis of the insane (GPI) who formed a fair proportion of the patients then in mental hospitals. It eventually turned out that GPI was a monogenic morbus whose pathological onset was a syphilitic infection. Since penicillin became available as a successful remedy of syphilis, the once so-common mental morbus of GPI has turned into a rarity.

The discovery of the neuropathological basis of GPI encouraged psychiatrists in their hope that other hitherto cryptogenic mental illnesses would turn out to be due to neuropathological diseases. Psychiatrists, therefore, talked freely at that time of nervous and mental 'diseases'. They believed that it was only a matter of time and painstaking research before psychiatric illnesses were put on the same footing as other medical illnesses which had already shed some of their cryptogenic uncertainties and acquired a more or less sound pathological basis.

Unfortunately, those hopes and beliefs were destined to disappointment. This had consequences of doubtful rationality. One can understand, and sympathize with, the impatience of the psychiatrists of the time who persuaded themselves that they could not wait until improved techniques might reveal the neuropathological changes they could not find. But it is not quite so easy to understand, and sympathize with, the unjustified conclusion that their negative findings meant that there was nothing to find, that functional psychiatric morbi had no disease components. One result of this conclusion was an embargo on the term 'disease'. Functional psychiatric morbi became known as 'disorders'. To diagnose a depressive 'disease' nowadays sounds almost like a solecism. In the psychopathic patients of today, what is thought to be affected is some disembodied mind which goes by the modern term of 'personality'. The patients concerned are said to have a 'psychopathic personality disorder'; they are even said to *be* 'psychopathic personalities', if one discounts the apparently irrelevant encumbrance of their bodies. To speak of a 'personality disease' might sound as much of a self-contradiction as the term 'square circle'.

Yet the circle had to be theoretically squared. This was achieved by an extension and re-evaluation of the concept of reflex arcs, viewing them as energy channels rather than solid structures. Originally, reflex arcs had been regarded as having their various centres in the spinal cord. But gradually the centres moved upward in the central nervous system, until they eventually reached cortical areas whose activities did not remain wholly unconscious, but had aspects which could be introspectively experienced.

This theoretical extension of reflex arcs to the highest cerebral centres had some unexpected by-products, when it was carried to uncompromising extremes. It removed from the concept of the brain the ability to instigate activities *de novo*. As a result, free will and personal responsibility went by the board. The brain's functions were believed to be initiated, controlled and moulded by the influx of stimuli

Molecular morbi

from the periphery. This would make personality a product of the environment. Such a possibility brought political interests into the arena and it inevitably followed that deep convictions and emotional commitments created controversies which rode roughshod over scholarly appraisals. Another by-product was linguistic. One hardly ever talks today of mental, psychological, or behavioural 'actions', but almost always of 'reactions' and 'responses'.

The reflex model seemed to offer a way of solving the conundrum of functional psychiatric disorders which originate in a structurally sound brain. The explanation could lie in the influx of conflicting stimuli, or rather of stimuli which need conflicting reflex discharges. There could then be a compromise discharge in the form of an unjustified emotional experience or an unnoticed maladroit action. There could also be a stalemate causing stimulus energy to be trapped in some region of the brain until an innocent stimulus set off an explosive discharge or until the accumulated energy found a circuitous escape route through abnormal channels, thus causing morbidly disordered functions.

The two main reflex theories which still hold the stage today are those evolved by Pavlov and Freud. The reflex basis was directly stated by Pavlov. He managed to produce disordered functions ('experimental neuroses') in animals, especially dogs, and explained them as due to 'an unusually acute clashing of the excitatory and inhibitory processes [in the brain], and the influence of strong and extraordinary stimuli [on it]' (Pavlov, 1926; translated and edited by Anrep, 1960, p. 297). He pictured the central nervous system as a reservoir of actual and potential reflex arcs. Some were inborn ('unconditioned') and others were acquired

The concepts of illness, disease and morbus

('conditioned') through learning from experience. In healthy organisms, there was a positive relation between the strength and kind of a stimulus and the strength and kind of the response to it. In neurotic organisms, there developed a tendency to respond to previously neutral stimuli ('stimulus generalization'), and the relation between stimulus and response could become 'paradoxical' in strength or 'ultraparadoxical' in kind.

Whereas Pavlov took great care to cast his theories into a purely physiological mould, avoiding and even vetoing all references to mental experiences, Freud deliberately tried to free himself from materialistic and anatomical fetters by introducing psychological concepts which were original and revolutionary. This obscured to some extent the origin of his theories in the reflex model. That they had such an origin can be clearly seen in his early writings. This has been fully elucidated by Ellenberger (1970, pp. 477f). Moreover, tell-tale materialistic and mechanistic phrases have remained in Freud's vocabulary. The mind of which he spoke was a 'mental apparatus' in which various 'mechanisms' could be activated. The mind was supplied with energy through stimuli from the environment and from the erotogenic zones of the body. The energy concerned was described as a 'sum, or amount of excitation, . . . [which] extends itself over the memory trace of an idea like an electric charge over the surface of the body' (Freud, 1894; *Collected Papers*, 1924, p. 75). This 'psychodynamic' energy was viewed as seeking discharge in thought, emotion, and action. When this was blocked by social or private taboos, discharge channels opened up which issued in sublimated, erroneous, or morbid psychological functions.

The reflex model of the brain which had inspired Pavlov

Molecular morbi

and Freud no longer holds the same explanatory appeal today. The electro-encephalogram has given clear evidence of brain activities which are obviously not dependent on the influx of stimuli, for example in deep sleep or under anaesthesia, and can be as autonomous as those of the pacemaker of the heart. Nor has the nervous system a prerogative in the creation of electric currents. All biochemical processes are accompanied by them. The electric impulses travelling along neuronal axons are initiated biochemically and are transmitted biochemically to other neurones, except during epileptic seizures.

The central nervous system is not alone either in its regulating and co-ordinating function of bodily processes. The endocrine and immune system share this function. It may thus be argued that the nervous system should be put on a par with the other systems and organs of the body. Whatever their various functions, they consist in, or are mediated by, biochemical processes in which globular protein molecules have a central role to play. Whereas, at one time, proteins were regarded as amorphous colloidal substances, we know today that they have specific, though complex, three-dimensional shapes. They are polypeptide chains which coil in upon themselves through covalent and non-covalent bonds which form between some of their amino-acid units. The polypeptide sequence of any protein is genetically determined because it is manufactured in the ribosomes of cells in accordance with chemically conveyed information from genes in the cell nucleus which had been activated for the purpose. The information contained in the genes is encoded in a nucleotide sequence that has been handed down through many cell divisions from the original nucleotide sequence in the zygote.

The concepts of illness, disease and morbus

The shape of globular protein molecules is, however, not steady. It undergoes continuous changes because their non-covalent bonds are affected by outside influences. In enzymes, for instance, the close presence of their specific substrates alters the shape of 'active' sites and initiates catalytic action. In addition, there are regulatory molecules which affect the shape of other enzyme areas which have been called 'allosteric' by Jacques Monod (Monod, Wyman & Changeux, 1965; Monod, 1972), and these shape changes have the effect of facilitating or inhibiting the functions of the active enzyme sites.

When the chemical composition of a globular protein molecule is wrong for genetic reasons or when its shape changes are seriously distorted in abnormal environments, we are dealing with structural pathological lesions of such small dimensions that most of them are beyond the resolving power of even the most effective electron microscope. If we extend the concept of Virchowian disease entities to include structural pathological lesions in protein molecules, then the distinction between functional disorders and organic diseases becomes void in the case of morbi based on what we may call 'proteinopathies'. Such proteinopathies may be monogenic disease entities, if they are derived from a morbid gene or gene pair so that pathological polypeptide chains are manufactured in the ribosomes of certain cells. But most proteinopathies are likely to be polygenic in origin and result from a variety of causes which distort the usual shape and the usual functional shape changes of a protein whose chemical composition is normal.

It cannot be denied that there is still a great deal of uncertainty and conjecture in this area of medicine which has only recently become accessible to research and presents

106

great technical difficulties. We have fairly full knowledge only about those proteinopathies which consist of pathological abnormalities of the haemoglobin molecule. It was Linus Pauling and his colleagues (Pauling, Itano, Singer & Wells, 1949) who noticed that patients with sickle-cell anaemia had haemoglobin which moved more slowly towards the positive pole of an electrophoretic field than the haemoglobin of healthy persons. The hypothesis was proposed that this difference was due to an altered chemical composition, and therefore an altered stereostructure, of the molecules of sickle-cell haemoglobin (HbS). Sickle-cell anaemia was labelled a 'molecular disease' by Pauling.

The first confirmation of this hypothesis came when Ingram (1956) demonstrated that the molecules of HbS had a wrong amino acid in the sixth position from the amino end of its two beta chains. The molecules of normal adult haemoglobin (HbA) had glutamic acid there, but HbS had valine instead. Glutamic acid is a polar molecule with a negative electric charge; valine, on the other hand, is a non-polar molecule, having no electric charge. The molecules of HbS therefore moved more slowly towards the positive pole of an electrophoretic field than the molecules of HbA.

Further confirmation came when Perutz (1964, 1967) finally succeeded after 23 years of research in establishing the stereostructure of haemoglobin and oxyhaemoglobin in almost complete detail. He could also show (Perutz & Lehmann, 1968) that HbS had an altered stereostructure, a 'molecular pathology' as he called it, which accounted for the abnormal sickle shapes of some erythrocytes in sickle-cell anaemia and their tendency to form long linear aggregates which can block small blood vessels.

The concepts of illness, disease and morbus

Although the stereostructure of other globular proteins, with the exception of myoglobin and of some small hydrolytic enzymes, is not yet known in much detail, there is already enough knowledge to postulate with sufficient confidence that cryptogenic morbi have as their pathological components molecular diseases in the form of proteinopathies. Such morbi may thus be called *'molecular morbi'*. It is because postulates of this kind have already gained much credence as far as the molecular morbi of the metabolic, endocrine, or immune systems are concerned, that the terms 'disorder' and 'disease' have tended to become interchangeable there.

This has not happened in the nosological fields of psychiatry and neurology. Yet there is no reason to assume that cryptogenic psychiatric and neurological morbi are essentially different from all other morbi. Indeed there is every reason to postulate that these morbi also have as their pathological components molecular diseases in the form of proteinopathies, that they also are molecular morbi. We know already that rapid changes in the permeability of neuronal membranes for sodium and potassium ions occur with the initiation and propagation of nervous impulses. Such rapid permeability changes are most likely to be due to rapid changes in the shape of globular proteins located in neuronal membranes. Similarly, the generation of neurotransmitter substances at nerve endings, their release into the synaptic cleft, and their inactivation or reabsorption must depend on the functions of globular proteins. Many of them are enzymes. Some of them have already been identified with the help of newly developed laboratory techniques, but most of them are still hidden from us.

We further know that the rate of protein synthesis in the

brain is as high as in the liver and higher than in any other organ of the body; and this despite the fact that the brain does not secrete large amounts of proteins. They are obviously required for the many functions occurring within the brain. Yet many, and perhaps most, of the proteins active in the brain are likely to be present in minute amounts only and have so far eluded detection. Some of the proteins must be specific to particular neurons, marking not only the individuality of a neuron, but also its place in a neuronal sequence. Mark (1974) has argued that it is such 'specific protein-containing marker molecules that maintain or modify . . . the detailed pattern of functional intercellular synaptic connections' (p. 98), i.e. that they are responsible for genetically determined neuronal connections and for the acquired modifications of such connections through learning and long-term memory functions.

The hypothesis of protein-containing marker molecules credits each neuron with the capacity of 'recognizing' other neurons by their marker molecules and being in turn 'recognized' by their own. Such mutual 'recognitions' between cells and even between extracellular protein molecules have already been noticed as characteristic features in the immune system. Indeed Jerne (1973) specifically pointed to the many similarities between the nervous and the immune systems. Both respond appropriately to an enormous variety of stimuli which can have an excitatory or inhibitory effect. Both systems form functional networks which adapt themselves to influences from the outside world. To quote Jerne: 'The ability of the axon of one neuron to form synapses with the correct set of other neurons must require something akin to epitope [marker molecule] recognition. Lymphocytes . . . move about freely. They too interact, however, either by direct encounters or through the anti-body molecules they release. These elements can recognize as well as be recognized, and in so doing they too form a network. As in the case of the nervous system, the modulation of the network by foreign signals represents its adaptation to the outside world. Both systems thereby learn from experience and build up a memory, a memory that is sustained by reinforcement but cannot be transmitted to the next generation'.

There may be loopholes in this analogy. Yet it points unmistakably to the fact that the nervous system is not alone in having mnestic, recognitive, and learning abilities, even if it is alone in having an introspective awareness of their results. Since these abilities are definitely mediated by globular proteins in the immune system, there is no justification for assuming that they must have a different basis in the nervous system. It would thus follow that the cryptogenic morbi of the nervous system may also be molecular morbi whose pathological components are proteinopathies of some kind. The last bastion of the distinction between functional disorders and organic diseases would thus fall. The nosological domain would uniformly consist of morbi of which many are still no more than taxonomic morbi of polygenic origin, though some have already achieved monogenic status. Yet we must keep in mind that monogenesis, to be of practical value, must be identifiable clinically through radical source indicators of a particular kind of pathological onset. Without such radical source indicators the monogenic origin of a morbus would be concealed in the welter of different pathological and clinical consequences that may spring from the same kind of pathological onset through the vagaries of adjuvant circumstances.

110

9

Summary

In pre-scientific times, diseases were reified and viewed as concrete entities which had their own independent existence. A version of this 'ontological' disease theory was propounded by Sydenham in the seventeenth century. For him, diagnostically important clinical manifestations in acute illnesses were attributes of the disease entity and not of the patient. Virchow espoused a different version of the ontological disease theory 200 years later. For him, a disease entity was a pathologically altered part of the body leading a parasitic existence in it. Since then, the notion of a disease entity has dropped the ontological requirement that an entity must have a more or less independent existence. Instead, the important feature of an entity has become the possession of a unitary and self-contained character. A disease entity in its modern sense has this character. It is viewed as a compound of morbid intra-organismic events which derives from a particular kind of *pathological onset*. A disease entity in its modern sense is thus a monogenic compound of events whose self-contained unity derives from the sameness of its pathological onset, even when it is otherwise composed of different pathological and clinical configurations. Events which can cause pathological onsets are differentiated as *noxae*. They occur in the spatio-temporal setting outside a patient's body, i.e. they temporally precede his existence or spatially impinge on him from his environment. We distinguish *unselective noxae* which

111

The concepts of illness, disease and morbus

always have pathological consequences and *selective noxae* which give rise to pathological consequences only, when special adjuvant circumstances prevail.

Most clinical configurations are causally overdetermined in that the same configuration can derive from different kinds of pathological abnormalities which are concomitant with it. Similarly, a pathological abnormality is causally overdetermined in that it can derive from different kinds of pathological onsets. To advance medical diagnostics, clinical manifestations are required which are to some extent not overdetermined, but monogenic. Such events have been called *source indicators*. The monogenicity of almost all clinical source indicators is limited in that they have, in normal circumstances, just one particular kind of pathological source which is concomitant with its clinical indicators, but is itself causally overdetermined through its derivation from different kinds of past pathological onsets. When the monogenicity of a source indicator is complete within the body of a patient so that it derives, in normal circumstances, from just one particular kind of known past pathological onset, then we call it a *radical source indicator*. In that case, we deal with a disease entity in its modern sense, i.e. with a monogenic disease entity.

Source indicators must be *valid* in that their source can be independently established by other means. They must be *reliable* in that they point, in normal circumstances, to just one particular kind of source. Source indicators vary in their *efficiency*, i.e. their ability to reveal details of their source.

Source indicators can fulfil their diagnostic functions only after they have been recognized with the help of those subjective perceptions whose veridicality can be objectively checked. Only exteroceptive and proprioceptive percep-

112

tions can serve this purpose. They are thus subjective source indicators which are, in favourable circumstances, valid, reliable, and highly efficient. Introspective perceptions are not among the subjective source indicators; they are no more than conscious experiences whose cerebral sources are still totally hidden from our knowledge. Nociceptive perceptions are clinically of great importance. They can be subjective source indicators; yet their validity, reliability, and efficiency are usually so poor that the establishment of their sources is a challenge to the expertise of the clinical diagnostician.

Clinical symptoms are events which can be perceived by the patient himself and/or his social environment. Most of them are not source indicators of their pathological origin. Clinical signs are events which are brought about and exterocepted in the course of a clinical investigation. They need not be source indicators of their pathological origin either. They become such source indicators only, when their validity, reliability, and efficiency in this respect have been established by research which usually involves investigations in non-clinical settings. Few clinical signs are radical source indicators. Only some of the diseases known to medicine today are therefore monogenic disease entities. This means that most of the classes of patients we differentiate nowadays are heterogeneous in their ultimate pathological origins.

To improve the classification of patients by a more judicious combination of the many clinical symptoms and signs known to us, perhaps with the help of statistical procedures, may have practical advantages, but it holds out little, if any, hope of finding new monogenic disease entities. Yet this hope is generally entertained. Why it is almost bound to be disappointed can be explained by a consideration of the logic of classes and classifications.

A class consists fundamentally of a collection of entities. They form the class members. In logical terminology, they are known as the class *extension*. It is a plurality except in the case of a unit class and the null class. The members of a class are chosen because they possess the same, or at least similar, classifying criteria. The compound totality of the classifying criteria of a class is known in logic as the *intension* of that class. It is an abstract entity by virtue of its unitary and self-contained character. A class can also be viewed as an abstract entity, namely as an *abstract class concept*, which unifies the usual plurality of class members and is of a higher type than they are so that it can never be a member of its own extension.

The three aspects of a class can be designated by different names. For example, the members of a particular class are known by the general name 'human being'. The intension of that class may be called 'humanity' or 'the attribute of being human'. The abstract class concept is known as 'mankind' or 'species *Homo sapiens*'.

We may distinguish two kinds of classes: empirical and theoretical (or non-empirical) ones. Empirical classes have as members concrete entities. For example, the empirical class of mammalian animals has as its members concrete living organisms, among them human beings. Theoretical classes have as members abstract entities. For example, the theoretical class of mammalian species has as its members abstract biological species, among them the species *Homo sapiens*, but not living organisms. A human being is a mammalian animal but not a mammalian species.

Logicians deal schematically with both kinds of classes. In

114

Summary

a strictly logical approach, classes have as their members entities which are devoid of any semantic meaning, such as the class of all entities x – whatever x may be. Classes of that kind are usually considered to be exactly demarcated so that an entity is either a member of a particular class or a non-member of it. Such exact demarcations are not necessarily found in the practical investigations of empirical or theoretical classes. It is then possible to encounter borderline entities whose membership in a particular class is a moot point which can be decided only arbitrarily.

The empirical domain (i.e. the universal class) of human beings can be divided into a class of patients and a class of non-patients. But these two classes are not complementary in a logical sense, because there are many borderline candidates of uncertain class membership. The intension of the class of patients is an abstract entity that may be called 'morbidity'. It is difficult to clarify the meaning of this entity and to establish the morbid attributes essential to it. The solution proposed here applies only to diagnosed or suspected human morbidity. It suggests that this morbidity is composed of attributes which are abnormal by population and/or individual standards and are also characterized by their ability to elicit therapeutic concern in the patients themselves and/or their social environment, as well as their ability to evoke medical concern in doctors. The concerns in question are subjective reactions in human beings and are thus influenced by cultural trends. Our classifying criteria for the class of human patients are therefore not absolute; they are merely pragmatic.

The concrete members of an empirical class are not identical in their appearance, they merely resemble each other because they exhibit the attributes listed in their class

115

intension only to some degree and to some extent. Their intensions are polythetic, i.e. they consist of several overlapping lists of attributes. Thus the members of empirical classes exhibit only a large proportion, or at least a significant portion, of all the attributes listed in the intension and these are exhibited to a varying degree.

The members of the universal class of patients therefore need only definitely exhibit a significant portion of the five kinds of attributes which compose morbidity in general, namely attributes which are abnormal by population and/or individual standards, which elicit therapeutic concern in the patients themselves and/or their social environment and which evoke medical concern.

If we take the universal class of patients as our domain, then the attributes of morbidity in general need no special mention, since they characterize all domain members. The domain of patients is divided into separate classes by different classifying criteria. A particular configuration of classifying criteria then constitutes the intension of a particular class of patients. If such a class appears homogeneous, its intension may be regarded as a particular disease. Since an intension is an abstract entity, there is a tendency to regard it as a disease entity. However, it is only a *taxonomic disease entity* whose composition is more or less arbitrary, even when it is firmly entrenched in medical theory and tradition. Taxonomic disease entities are, for the most part, of mere classificatory convenience. Most of them are polygenic in their pathological origins. Only very few are monogenic, because their pathological onset has already been detected and there are radical source indicators among their clinical manifestations. Only very few are thus disease entities in a modern sense.

116

Summary

We do not always deal in medicine with concrete patients and the empirical classes to which they belong. In medical theories and publications, we deal with abstract entities. Foremost among them are taxonomic disease entities. They are among the individual members of the nosological domain. This is a theoretical domain. Yet not all the members in it can be regarded as taxonomic disease entities. The reason for this is that through the influence of Virchow the term *disease* has acquired a narrowed technical sense. It has come to signify, more or less exclusively, configurations of pathological abnormalities. If this narrowed sense is accepted, and this has been largely the case, a special term is needed to designate configurations of clinical manifestations. The term *illness* has been adopted for this purpose. We could then say that the members of the nosological domain are taxonomic disease and/or illness entities. This would be a bit cumbersome, however. It has therefore been proposed to use the term *morbus* to designate a unifying concept which has, in theory at least, both an illness and a disease component. It must, however, be kept in mind that the ultimate aim of modern diagnostics is the establishment of morbi which are not just taxonomic entities, not just products of a more-or-less arbitrary classification, but are monogenic entities which derive their unitary and self-contained character from their causal origin in a particular kind of pathological onset. Unfortunately, most of the morbi accepted in modern medicine are only taxonomic entities whose causal derivation is merely partially known and therefore polygenic.

Most morbi begin their nosological career as cryptogenic illnesses. The name applied to them may have been derived from some conspicuous clinical symptom or from some

The concepts of illness, disease and morbus

aetiological speculations. Some of these ill-founded names have survived through centuries of medical history, during which they often changed their meanings. Whenever this happened, the classes they characterized had different kinds of patients as members. Even names of a more recent coinage are not too definite in their meanings. Indeed they may be highly equivocal, sometimes capable of signifying ambiguously a clinical manifestation or an illness or a disease or a morbus as a whole. The context in which they are used may prevent confusion, but not always.

Virchowian views put a premium on the diagnostic significance of structural pathological lesions. Morbid changes of functions were supposed to be the result of such lesions. This presented clinicians with the awkward problem of explaining morbidly altered functions in the absence of structural pathological lesions. The explanations put forward relied on hazy notions of metabolic processes or on near-mythical ideas about the nature of nervous energy and the manner in which it activated and regulated bodily activities. The result was that morbi were divided into two kinds: those which had structural lesions as their pathological components and those which had not. The pathological components of the former were called *organic diseases*, those of the latter *functional disorders*.

This differentiation between organic diseases and functional disorders has been gradually blurred by modern advances in biochemical knowledge and the realization of the extent to which biological functions are mediated by minute stereomolecular shape changes in globular proteins. If those shape changes are pathologically abnormal, they constitute *molecular diseases* and these can form the basis of morbid disorders of metabolic, endocrine, immunological,

118

Summary

neurological, psychological, and other biological functions. The result has been that, in many nosological areas, functional disorders have been put on a par with organic diseases. In those areas, the tendency has emerged to use the terms 'disorder' and 'disease' interchangeably. Only in neurological and psychiatric morbi has this distinction survived. This survival is partly due to beliefs that some biological functions are non-material in origin and partly due to a fundamental lack of knowledge in certain biological fields which have not yet yielded their secrets to the efforts of modern research.

References

Ackerknecht, E. H. (1953). *Rudolf Virchow. Doctor, Statesman, Anthropologist.* Madison: University of Wisconsin Press

Armstrong, D. M. (1968). *A Materialist Theory of the Mind.* London: Routledge & Kegan Paul

Beard, G. M. (1869). Neurasthenia, or nervous exhaustion. *Boston Med. Surg. J.* **3,** 217–21

Beard, G. M. (1880). *A Practical Treatise on Nervous Exhaustion (Neurasthenia), Its Symptoms, Nature, Sequence, Treatment.* New York: W. Wood

Berghoff, E. (1947). Entwicklungsgeschichte des Krankheitsbegriffes. In *Wiener Beitraege zur Geschichte der Medizin.* Vienna: Wilhelm Maudrich

Carnap, R. (1956). *Meaning and Necessity. A Study in Semantics and Modal Logic:* enlarged edition. University of Chicago Press

Cecil-Loeb's Textbook of Medicine. (1971). 13th edn. Ed. P. B. Beeson & W. McDermott. Philadelphia, London, Toronto: W. B. Saunders

Clendening, L. (1942). *Source Book of Medical History.* New York: Dover Publications

Cullen, W. (1772). *Nosology, or a Systematic Arrangement of Diseases by Classes, Orders, Genera, and Species with the Distinguishing Characteristics of Each.* Edinburgh

Cullen, W. (1777). *First Lines of the Practice of Physic.* London

Dewhurst, K. (1966). *Dr Thomas Sydenham (1624–1689). His Life and Original Writings.* London: The Wellcome Historical Medical Library

Doran, F. S. A. (1967). *The Lancet,* **3,** 1204

Du Bois-Reymond, E. (1843). Vorläufiger Abriss einer Untersuchung über den sogenannten Froschstrom und über die elektromotorischen Fische. *Ann. Physik und Chemie,* **1,** 58. (Quoted from Brazier, M. A. B. (1958). The Evolution of Con-

References

cepts Relating to Electrical Activity of the Nervous System. 1600–1800.) In *The Brain and Its Functions*. A Symposium, pp. 191–220. Oxford: Blackwell

Eddington, Sir A. (1935). *The Nature of the Physical World*. London: J. M. Dent

Ellenberger, H. F. (1970). *The Discovery of the Unconscious. The History and Evolution of Dynamic Psychiatry*. London: Penguin Books

Entralgo, P. L. (1955). *Mind and Body. Psychosomatic Pathology: A Short History of the Evolution of Medical Thought*. London: Harvill

Faber, K. (1930). *Nosography. The Evolution of Clinical Medicine in Modern Times*. New York: Paul B. Hoeber

Farr, W. (1856). Report on the nomenclature and statistical classification of diseases for statistical returns. In *Sixteenth Annual Report of the Registrar General*. London: Longman, Brown, Green & Longmans

Feinstein, A. R. (1967). *Clinical Judgment*. Baltimore, Md: The Williams & Wilkins Company

Fölling, A. (1934). Ueber Ausscheidung von Phenylbrenztraubensaeure in den Harn als Stoffwechselanomalie in Verbindung mit Imbezillitaet. *Hoppe-Zeiler's Z. Physiol. Chem.* **227**, 169–76

Frege, G. (1879). *Begriffsschrift, eine der arithmetischen nachgebildete Formelsprache des reinen Denkens*. Hall (*See also* Geach & Black, 1952.)

Freud, S. (1894). The defence neuro-psychoses. In *Collected Papers*, Vol. I. (1924). London: Hogarth Press

Geach, P. & Black, M. (eds). (1952). *Translations from the Philosophical Writings of Gottlob Frege*. Oxford

Graves, R. (1955). *The Greek Myths*. London: Penguin Books

Hamilton, Sir W. (1860). *Lectures on Logic*, ed. H. L. Mansel & J. Veitch. Edinburgh. (Quoted from Kneale & Kneale, 1964.)

Hume, D. (1739). *A Treatise of Human Nature*. Oxford

Ingram, V. M. (1956). A specific chemical difference between the globins of normal human and sickle-cell anaemia haemoglobin. *Nature*, London, **178**, 792–94

Jerne, N. K. (1973). The immune system. *Scientific American*, **229**, 52–60

References

Kendell, R. E. (1975a). The concept of disease and its implications for psychiatry. *Brit. J. Psychiatry*, **127**, 305–15

Kendell, R. E. (1975b). *The Role of Diagnosis in Psychiatry*. Oxford: Blackwell

Kendell, R. E., Cooper, J. E., Gourlay, A. J., Copeland, J. R. M., Sharpe, L. & Gurland, B. J. (1971). The diagnostic criteria of American and British psychiatrists. *Arch. gen. Psychiatry*, **25**, 123–30

Kneale, W. & Kneale, M. (1964). *The Development of Logic*. Oxford

Körner, S. (1966). *Experience and Theory. An Essay in the Philosophy of Science*. London: Routledge & Kegan Paul

Laplace, P. S. (1814). Essai philosophique sur les probabilitès. In *Théorie Analitique des Probabilités*. 2nd edn, English Translation: *A Philosophical Essay on Probabilities*, F. W. Truscott & F. L. Emory (1902). New York

Latham, R. G. (1848). *Thomas Sydenham: Works*. Translated from the Latin edition of Dr Greenhill. London: Sydenham Society

Mark, R. (1974). *Memory and Nerve Cell Connections. Criticisms and Contributions from Developmental Neurophysiology*. Oxford: Clarendon Press.

Molière, J. P. P. (1665). *L'Amour Médecin*. (Quoted from Clendening, 1942.)

Monod, J. (1972). *Chance and Necessity. An Essay on the Natural Philosophy of Modern Biology*. London: Collins

Monod, J., Wyman, J. & Changeux, J. P. (1965). On the nature of allosteric transition. A plausible model. *J. mol. Biol.*, **12**, 88–118

Munn, A. M. (1960). *Free-Will and Determinism*. London: MacGibbon & Kee

Newton, Sir I. (1713). *General Scholium*. (Quoted from Wightman, 1958.)

O'Connor, J. (ed.) (1969). *Modern Materialism: Readings on Mind-Body Identity*. New York: Harcourt, Brace & World

Pauling, L., Itano, H. A., Singer, S. J. & Wells, I. C. (1949). Sickle-cell anemia, a molecular disease. *Science*, Washington, **110**, 543–8

Pavlov, I. P. (1926). *Conditioned Reflexes. An Investigation of the Physiological Activity of the Cerebral Cortex*. Translated and edited by G. V. Anrep (1960). New York: Dover Publications

References

Penrose, L. S. & Quastel, J. H. (1937). Metabolic studies in phenyl-ketonuria. *Biochem. J.*, **31**, 266–74

Penrose, L. S. & Smith, G. F. (1966). *Down's Anomaly*. London: J. & A. Churchill

Perutz, M. F. (1964). The hemoglobin molecule. *Scientific American*, **211**, 64–76

Perutz, M. F. (1967). Some molecular controls in biology. *Endeavour*, **26**, 3

Perutz, M. F. & Lehmann, H. (1968). Molecular pathology of human haemoglobin. *Nature, London*, **219**, 902

Piaget, J. (1955). *The Construction of Reality in the Child*. London: Routledge & Kegan Paul

Popper, Sir K. R. (1973). *Objective Knowledge. An Evolutionary Approach*. Oxford: Clarendon Press

Price's Textbook of the Practice of Medicine. 11th edn. (1973). Ed. Sir R. Bodley Scott. London: Oxford University Press

Quine, W. V. (1961). Mathematical Logic. Cambridge, Mass.: Harvard University Press

Rather, L. J. (1959). Harvey, Virchow, Bernard and the Methodology of Science. In *Virchow, Disease, Life and Man. Selected Essays by Rudolf Virchow*, ed. L. J. Rather. Stanford: University Press

Russell, B. (1937). *The Principles of Mathematics*. 2nd edn. London: George Allen & Unwin

Russell, B. (1961). *History of Western Philosophy and its Connection with Political and Social Circumstances from the Earliest Times to the Present Day*. London: George Allen & Unwin

Scadding, J. G. (1967). Diagnosis: the clinician and the computer. *The Lancet*, **2**, 877–82

Singer, C. & Underwood, E. A. (1962). *A Short History of Medicine*. Second edition. Oxford: Clarendon Press

Sneath, P. H. A. (1962). The construction of taxonomic groups. In *Microbial Classification, 12th Symposium of the Society for General Microbiology*, eds. G. C. Ainsworth & P. H. A. Sneath. Cambridge University Press

Sokal, R. R. & Sneath, P. H. A. (1963). *Principles of Numerical Taxonomy*. San Francisco & London: W. H. Freeman

Sushruta Samhitá. Translated and edited by K. K. Bhishagratna

References

(1907–16). Varanasi-1, India: The Chowkamba Sanskrit Series Office, 1963

Sydenham, T. (1676). *Works.* (*See* Latham, 1848.)

Taylor, F. Kräupl (1966) *Psychopathology. Its Causes and Symptoms.* London: Butterworths–Revised edition, (1979). London: Quartermaine House

Taylor, F. Kräupl (1971). A logical analysis of the medico-psychological concept of disease. Part 1. *Psycholog. Med.,* **1,** 356–64

Taylor, F. Kräupl (1972). A logical analysis of the medico-psychological concept of disease. Part 2. *Psycholog. Med.,* **2,** 7–16

Taylor, F. Kräupl (1976). The medical model of the disease concept. *Brit. J. Psychiatry,* **128,** 588–94

Thiel, C. (1972). Gottlob Frege: Die Abstraktion. In *Grundprobleme der Grossen Philosophen. Philosophie der Gegenwart I,* ed. J. Speck. Göttingen: Vandenhoeck & Ruprecht

Virchow, R. (1847). Ueber die Standpunkte in der wissenschaftlichen Medizin. *Virchow's Archiv fuer Pathologische Anatomie und Physiologie und fuer Klinische Medizin,* **1,** 3–19

Virchow, R. (1849). Die naturwissenschaftliche Methode und die Standpunkte in der Therapie. *Virchow's Archiv fuer Pathologische Anatomie und Physiologie und fuer Klinische Medizin,* **2,** 3–37

Virchow, R. (1858). *Cellular Pathology.* Translated by F. Chance (1860). Philadelphia

Virchow, R. (1895). *Hundert Jahre Allgemeine Pathologie.* Berlin

Webster's *Third New International Dictionary of the English Language.* Springfield, Mass.: G. & C. Merriam Company

Whitehead, A. N. & Russell, B. (1927). *Principia Mathematica.* Second edition. Cambridge University Press

Wightman, W. P. D. (1958). Wars of ideas in neurological science – from Willis to Bichat and from Locke to Condillac. In *The History and Philosophy of Knowledge of the Brain and its Functions.* Oxford: Blackwell

World Health Organization (1973). *The International Pilot Study of Schizophrenia.* Geneva

Ziegenfuss, W. (194950). *Philosophen-Lexikon. Handwoerterbuch der Philosophie nach Personen.* (Quoted from C. Thiel, 1972, q.v.).

Name Index

Index

O'Connor, J., 40
Ord, W. M., 84

Pasteur, L., 80
Pauling, L., 107
Pavlov, I. P., 103, 104
Penrose, L. S., 24, 84
Perutz, M. F., 107
Piaget, J. I., 1
Popper, Sir Karl, 22

Quastel, J. H., 84
Quine, W. V., 90

Rather, L. J., 11
Reinhardt, B., 11
Roscellin, 86
Russell, B., 46, 48, 89, 90

Scadding, J. G., 65f., 91
Shepherd, M., 94
Singer, C., 84
Singer, S. J., 107

Smith, G. F., 24
Sneath, P. H. A., 55, 56
Sokal, R. R., 55
Sydenham, T., 6f., 14, 17f., 86, 111

Taylor, F. Kräupl, 63, 68f.
Thiel, C., 48

Underwood, E. A., 84

Virchow, R., 11f., 15, 17f., 74, 76,
    100, 111, 117, 118
Volta, A., 99

Wells, I. C., 107
Whitehead, A. N., 89, 90
Wightman, W. P. D., 97
William of Occam, 86
Willis, T., 43
Wöhler, F., 96
Wyman, J., 106

Ziegenfuss, W., 48

Subject Index

abnormality, 61
  by individual or population
    standards (norms) 63, 115
action currents, 99
ague, 82
animal electricity, 98
axiom of non-contradiction, 51

bacteriology, 18
belonging, relation of, 47
biochemistry, 99, 118
'Brunonian' theory, 98

casuality, 1, 21
cause
  necessary, 23
  pathological, 77, 83
  sufficient, 23
circumstances, adjuvant, 24, 110,
  112
class, 46, 114
  as one, 46
  as many, 47
  biological, 54
  comprehension of, 50
  concept, 46, 114
  empirical, 46, 114
  empty, 47
  entity, 46, 114
  exact, 52, 115
  extension of, 47, 49f., 114
  homogeneity of, 73
  inexact, 52
  intension of, 51, 59, 114
  and logicians, 46, 114
  names of, 88, 114
  non-empirical, 46

null, 47
plurality, 46
resemblance, 52
sub-class, 48, 52
super-class, 48
theoretical, 46, 78, 114
unit, 47
unity, 46, 114
class homogeneity
  causal derivation of, 73
  taxonomic, 73
classification, 54f., 114
  intensional, 58
  ostensive, 57
classifying criterion, 73, 81, 114, 116
concept, 86
  nosological, 87
conceptualism, scholastic, 86, 90
containment, relation of, 48
'cretinoid condition of middle-aged
  women', 84
cybernetics, 29

degeneracy, 2
determinism, scientific, 22
diabetes, 43
  insipidus, 44
  mellitus, 44
  renal, 43
diphtheria, 19
disadvantage, biological 65ff.
disease, 73ff., 117
  asthenic, 98
  International Classification of
    (ICD), 79
  mental, 101
  molecular, 107, 108, 119

Index

Index

Index

Index